HELP … I'M LEADING WORSHIP!

HELP ...
I'M LEADING WORSHIP!

CHURCH OF SCOTLAND
WOMAN'S GUILD

SAINT ANDREW PRESS
EDINBURGH

First published in 1994 by
SAINT ANDREW PRESS
121 George Street, Edinburgh EH2 4YN

on behalf of
The CHURCH of SCOTLAND WOMAN'S GUILD

Copyright © Church of Scotland Woman's Guild 1994

ISBN 0 86153 197 3

British Library Cataloguing in Publication Data
A catalogue record for this book
is available from the British Library.

ISBN 0861531973

Cover design by Mark Blackadder.
Cover photograph by Paul Turner.
Printed and bound by Hugh K. Clarkson & Sons Ltd, West Calder

CONTENTS

INTRODUCTION   vii
DEDICATION and KEY TO ABBREVIATIONS   viii
ACKNOWLEDGMENTS   ix
LEADING WORSHIP   1
SOMETHING DIFFERENT!   4
ABOUT PRAYER   9
ADDRESSING GOD   13
PRAYERS
    … of Adoration   16
    … of Confession   18
    … of Thanksgiving   21
    … for Others and Ourselves   23
    Offering Prayers   28
    Closing Prayers   30
    Benedictions   33
    … at the Beginning of a New Session   35
    … for the Guild   37
    Classic Prayers   39
    Favourite Prayers   41
    … from around the World   43
    Paraphrase and Prayer based on 1 Corinthians 13   45
    An Outline Prayer   49
ANOTHER WAY TO PRAY
    Contemplation of the Gospels   52
    Introductory Exercise in Contemplation 55
    Contemplation of a Gospel Passage   58
    Meditation on Violence   61

THE PSALMS
    The Prayer Book of Jesus   64
    Praying through the Psalms   68
A GUIDE TO BIBLE READINGS   72
SUGGESTIONS FOR USING THE BIBLE   76
WORSHIP SAMPLER   86
    The Fruit of the Spirit is
        … Love   87
        … Joy and Peace   89
        … Patience and Kindness   91
        … Goodness   93
        … Faithfulness   94
        … Humility and Self-control   96
SAMPLE PATTERNS
        … Beginnings   99
        … Caring   100
        … Celebration   102
        … Communication   104
        … Family   107
        … Grief/Loss   108
        … The Media   111
        … Missed Opportunities   116
        … Relationships   119
        … Salt in Society   120
        … Wisdom   122
        Christmas   123
        New Year   125
        Lent   126
        Annual General Meeting   128
        'Whose I am and Whom I Serve'   130
        Epilogue for World Mission   133
        An Epilogue with a Challenge   135
THE CENTENARY HYMN   137
REFERENCES   139
RESOURCES   140

INTRODUCTION

Worshipping together is an integral ingredient of Woman's Guild meetings. What joy it brings to our members to praise and pray as they meet in fellowship. Presidents and delegates gladly give time, thought and prayers as they prepare them-selves for the awesome responsibility of leading worship.

This book is designed to be of help to all those who are asked to lead worship. It comes as a supplement to *Fresh Ideas for Worship*, so beloved and so well used by countless Guild members over recent years. I know it will be warmly welcomed by our members and I commend its use in our Branches and Groups.

May God bless our worship and our witness and to him be the glory.

Mary S Sherrard
National President, WOMAN'S GUILD
February 1994

DEDICATION

This book is dedicated to the members of the Church of Scotland Woman's Guild, both in Branch and Young Woman's Group. Some of those using it may be preparing to lead worship in a meeting for the first time, while others may have considerable experience in that field of service. We hope that each may find something to guide or inspire in these pages.

Warmest thanks are due to all those who have given so freely of their time, expertise and guidance in the production of this book.

KEY TO ABBREVIATIONS

CH3	=	*Church Hymnary* (third edition)
JP	=	*Junior Praise*
MP	=	*Mission Praise* (numbered as in individual volumes)
SGP	=	*Songs of God's People*
SHF	=	*Songs and Hymns of Fellowship* (Integrated edition)
AV	=	*Authorised Version*
GNB	=	*Good News Bible*
JB	=	*Jerusalem Bible*
NEB	=	*New English Bible*
NIV	=	*New International Version*

ACKNOWLEDGMENTS

The Church of Scotland Woman's Guild would like to express its appreciation and gratitude to the following sources for material used in this publication:

Church of Scotland Department of National Mission (page 6); David Adam (p 39), from *Edge of Glory* (SPCK/Triangle, 1985); David Adam (p 42), from *Tides and Seasons* (SPCK/ Triangle, 1989); Freda Rajotte (p 42), 'Tourist's Prayer' from *With all God's People: The New Ecumenical Prayer Cycle*, John Carden (comp), (WCC Publications, 1989); Rosaleen Murray (p 42) (Scottish Catholic International Aid Fund); Bishop Desmond Tutu (p 44); Eddie Askew (p 97), from *Breaking the Rules* (Leprosy Mission International); SPAN (*Service – Prayer and News*) for Presbyterian Women in NSW, Australia (p 100); Jane Grayshon (p 120), from *Faith in Flames* (Hodder & Stoughton, 1990); M Louise Haskins (p 125), from *The Desert* (*c.* 1908); Wild Goose Worship Group (p 127), from *A Wee Worship Book* (The Iona Community); John C Sharp and John Wilson (p 135), from *Life is for Everyone* (Saint Andrew Press, 1988); © Betty Ewart (p 137).

Thanks are also due to the members of the Woman's Guild who submitted material for inclusion in this publication and to all those who gave most generously of their time and effort.

LEADING WORSHIP

WHY do we worship?

Worship is an essential part of the life of the Christian church. It gives us an opportunity to draw near to God to worship and honour him; to praise and thank him for all his goodness; to seek his forgiveness and pardon; to bring our requests and petitions to him; and to be still and know that he is God.

It is not surprising then that the acts of worship and devotion form an essential part of our meetings. It is an awesome thing for us to enter into the presence of God, and we all feel unworthy, but Jesus Christ has shown us the way, and through him we can know the peace of being in the presence of the Lord, and accepted by him.

It is not a thing to fear, for we are coming to a loving God, who wants us to be with him and to spend time with him. He knows our misgivings, but is ready to help and enable us in all we seek to do for him.

Often we hear the comment, 'What right have I to lead our meeting in prayer? ... I'm not good enough'. If you are reading this book seeking help, then you are probably already in the position of being asked to lead the act of worship. Having been asked means that God is opening a door for you to draw nearer to him in faith – he is waiting to meet you and help you.

WHEN should it take place?

For our meetings to be real times of fellowship, worship must be present. Whether the act of worship comes at the beginning or end (or even in the middle) of the meeting is dependent on the format of the meeting. There is no set time.

HOW do we set about it?

There are differing types and styles of worship – you must choose the most appropriate one and the one with which you feel comfortable and happy. However, try to keep it from being the same each week – variations are a good thing. Consider the meeting itself – the theme, the speaker, those who will be present and their needs, and anything else which would influence the atmosphere of the meeting. With these thoughts in your mind decide on the style and type of worship.

WHAT should it include?

It helps to create a sense of worship if there is a focal point – flowers, or a candle, or an open Bible on the table. If you have an epilogue then a few moments of quiet music can help to calm the atmosphere and give a sense of God's peace.

The worship time might include readings, prayers, singing and slides – it is therefore a wise thing to involve others in this task. This also gives to other members an opportunity to grow in their faith and experience.

Don't leave your preparation to the last minute – things invariably crop up and panic can set in!

MUSIC: for many people music is an important part of worship and it can allow members to use their gifts – vocal or instrumental. Don't be afraid to sing unaccompanied! Many new hymns or songs lend themselves to this (examples can be found in *Songs of God's People*). Be imaginative in your choice! Members may welcome the chance to try something new as well as the traditional favourites and there is plenty of new material available.

PRAYERS: this time for drawing near to God is a great privilege. Speak with God in simple, ordinary, every day language. God will lovingly accept your prayers and your members will understand them and feel a part of them. There is no special virtue in long prayers. Take time to prepare them, think through what you want them to say and pray them from your heart. Always remember that God is waiting to meet with us at any time, in any place, and he will answer our prayers. Having accepted this act of leadership as a lesson in faith, commit yourself and your task to God and he will bless you.

SOMETHING DIFFERENT!

Be adventurous in worship! Why not try some of the following ideas as part of your meeting? Be sensitive though, as with planning all worship it is important to tailor things to fit in with the rest of the evening's programme.

READING: a fresh approach to Bible reading is to have two or more readers. They need not necessarily stand at the front; sometimes it is more effective for the 'voices' to come from the midst of the audience/congregation; or from behind (but be sure they can be heard!).

Some passages lend themselves particularly well to this approach: *eg* the temptations of Jesus in Matthew 4: 1 - 11. This could be read by five voices: one as narrator, one as the voice of Jesus and one for each of the three temptations.

Some of the Psalms are effective read in this way: *eg* Psalm 13 – three voices could be used for the three stanzas (verses 1, 2; 3, 4; 5, 6).

DRAMA: this can be used to great effect. There are many good resources available on Christian themes, some giving adaptations or re-telling of Bible stories. If you are going to use drama, make sure you have time to rehearse. Keep it simple – try to avoid complicated staging or elaborate props – and bear in mind how the drama is to fit in with the rest of the worship.

Useful material includes:

- – Bell and Maule: *Wild Goose prints* (vols 1 - 6)
- – Burbridge & Watts: *Time to Act*
- – Burbridge & Watts: *Lightning Sketches*
- – *Dramatised Bible*

MIME and CLOWNING: these are increasingly used in contemporary worship. Mime could be used to illustrate a story: *eg* the Parable of the Pharisee and the Tax Collector (Luke 18: 9 - 14). Two actors could demonstrate the contrast in attitude of the two men.

Mime can be used to highlight the message of a particular piece of music or a song: *eg* 'Father we adore you'. Perhaps two or three people could perform these three simple movements:

(1) 'Father we adore you' – arms raised in adoration
(2) 'Lay our lives before you' – arms out, 'offering' our lives
(3) 'How we love you' – arms crossed over chest

Remember when you are using mime that it is particularly important that the performers can be easily seen.

In some areas of the country there are individuals and groups who specialise in Clown ministry. Perhaps you could invite one of them to take part in your meeting.

ACTION PRAYER: if you would like to involve all of your group, here is a simple Action Prayer to try:

Lord, here are my hands! Help me to see them as you see them	– Hold hands out in front of you.
When I am angry …	– Clench fists and shake them.
make me calm	– Hands on breast.
When I am sad …	– Bury face in hands and bow yourself forward.
make me joyful	– Stretch up arms and spread hands outwards.
When I am greedy	– Make hands like grasping claws.
make me generous	– Turn hands over, palms open and up.
When I am frightened	– Hands up to face, palms out, screening face.
give me peace	– Hands in gesture of prayer.

~ *Windows of Prayer*[1] ~

A useful book for both mime and dance is *Steps of Faith*[2] by Geoffrey and Judith Stevenson.

DANCE: this can be used in worship either by a small group (here it may overlap with mime: see 'Father, we adore you' above) or involving everyone. A simple dance for the start of a new session or for a joint meeting is the 'Greet Dance'.

Participants form a circle and join hands. (If numbers are sufficient, form two circles, one inside the other – like a 'Paul Jones'. The circles will then move in opposite directions to greet each other.) To appropriate music, the circle moves round slowly, using a simple step pattern such as:

(1) Step forward on right foot
    Bring left foot forward beside right
    Bend knees (down, up – in time to music)

(2) Step back on right foot
    Bring left foot back beside right
    Bend knees

(3) Side-step to the right (move right foot to the right,
    bring left foot alongside it) three times
    Bend knees

Repeat steps (1) to (3) as often as desired.

Once the steps have been learned (without music to begin with) explain the symbolism:

(1) We step forward to greet and acknowledge each other.

(2) We step back to take our place as members of the group.

(3) We move round together as witness to the importance of the unity of the group as part of the body of Christ.

There is a wide range of suitable music including 'Jubilate Deo' or 'You shall go out with joy' (SGP). If there is no pianist or tape available, participants could sing either of these while using the dance, and any members of your group not able to dance could still join in by contributing to the music.

VISUAL ARTS: these can be used as a backdrop for worship. A poster, picture or banner can be a focus for silent meditation.

An extension of this idea is to use a series of slides as part of worship. These could tie in with the theme of the meeting. For instance, pictures of flowers, countryside, even litter, could be used as a prelude to a discussion on 'caring for creation'. Music (appropriate sacred or secular) can be used in the background; or the pictures could lead into prayer and meditation.

Something different in worship will require prayerful thought and careful preparation beforehand. Clear explanations of what is planned will be needed, especially if the audience/ congregation is expected to take part. But it can be a very enriching experience for all. Let us 'sing a new song to the Lord'!

ABOUT
PRAYER

'Yes, of course I'll do a reading for you – just don't ask me to say a prayer!' As Guild Presidents up and down the country are well aware, when it comes to sharing worship in the Branch or Group, members will volunteer to read quite readily, or may be prepared to lead the meeting, but praying is something different.

A member of a Guild committee went to a training course, full of expectation, having more time to give to the Guild – and returned downhearted. The reason? 'Someone said praying in public should be no problem – the Lord will give you the words as you speak.' The committee member believed she could never do this and so felt a failure as a committee member – and even as a Christian.

There are two sides to this question. Extempore or spontaneous prayers can be beautiful, meaningful and just right for the occasion. Equally, however, prayers written by many different people, whether famous or anonymous, can be read to great effect, as can the leader's own prepared prayers. None of these methods is 'right' or 'wrong'. None is more Christian or more devout than another. They are all different and God can use them all in his service and to his glory. There are differences in worship and different styles of prayer which vary a great deal within our churches. Some are used to informal, spontaneous times of prayer; some are used to formal language and quite rigid orderings of content; still others would see it as the minister's right to lead a meeting in prayer.

Out of all this, as a Guild, we have a commitment, gladly stated in our Aim, to unite in worship. So what does that mean in practice? *Do* we pray at our meetings? Do we pray at *all* our meetings? We believe in a God who is ever present, caring and interested in all we do. Yet so often when we have a fun meeting, a social, an entertainment, we leave him out and don't acknowledge his presence! Are we ashamed of having fun? Is such a meeting not suitable for prayer? Who gave us the capacity to have fun and enjoyment? Let's be publicly thankful – not just to the entertainers and the tea committee!

From this, however, we realise that prayers will not always be similar in content. There are times and occasions when standard prayers will be needed – opening a meeting, dedicating an offering and closing a meeting. At other times, prayers will be adapted to the content of the meeting for the evening – praying for caring organisations, giving praise for the beauty of the world around us, asking for help in understanding our faith. Prayers can be long or short, led by a leader or other member, written out by the person praying or compiled from different sources.

For many people, the Guild has been a training ground in prayer – private and public – and it is important that we continue this tradition by encouraging and helping members to share in public worship. God will give us the words, but these words can come from many different places and at different times – not just through his Spirit as we rise to our feet – though that may well be the most natural way for some. Many of us, for public worship, need the assurance of some help, some written words to ensure that, as Paul said, we 'let all things be done decently and in good order'. This is especially important when we lead others in worship and to honour God by approaching him with reverence and with dignity.

The prayers in this section are offered as an aid to worship in Guild meetings and as a guide to prayers of our own. They include prayers of adoration, confession, thanksgiving, intercession and petition, and you may choose to follow that structure, or adapt it to suit your needs. There are also prayers for specific times or events, and well-known prayers that have enriched worship down through the centuries and in many parts of the world.

On a practical level, prayers should have a beginning, a middle and an end! That may seem to state the obvious, but sometimes the beginnings and endings can cause problems. It is important to give clear signals about these when leading worship in public. The members of the group should be told when the prayer is about to begin so that they can be ready to take part by listening. The simple words 'Let us pray' are all that is required, though you may prefer another form. If there are to be pauses for silent prayers, or if the group is to be invited to join in responsively, this should be made clear before you begin.

Similarly at the end the prayer should be brought to a definite close. As Christians we offer our prayers through, or in the name of our Lord Jesus Christ, so use a phrase such as 'All these things we ask in the name of Jesus Christ, our Lord. *Amen.*'

These simple signals allow the audience to join meaningfully in the prayer as listeners, because they know what to expect and what is expected of them.

We all pray – when we're happy, when we are sad, when we're in trouble, for others in trouble. For the Christian, prayer should be as natural as breathing; it is our life-line to God and the powerhouse from which we gain strength and support for ourselves and for others. So, whether we find praying easy or whether we need help; whether we have been Christians for five years or fifty; whether we enjoy leading worship or whether we would rather do anything else, these prayers are offered with confident hope that God will bless their use and bless all those who make use of them in worship. We come with the same request as Jesus' disciples did so many years ago: 'Lord, teach us to pray'.

ADDRESSING GOD

How do we begin? How should we address God? If these questions worry you, perhaps the suggestions below may help.

When we look at The Lord's Prayer, we find that Jesus taught his followers to speak to God simply and directly, as a child talking to a parent – 'Our Father in heaven'. So our approach should be simple and natural, while still being reverent.

In the regular conduct of worship at meetings, we may want to focus on particular aspects of the nature of God that are appropriate on different occasions: *eg* 'Bountiful God, Creator of all things' at time of Harvest Thanksgiving; or 'Eternal God, Ruler of all the World' at the approach to the World Day of Prayer.

It may also be useful to remember that God is revealed and worshipped as Father, Son and Holy Spirit. Our prayers can sometimes concentrate on one or more of these: *eg* the various names of Jesus at Christmas or Easter – 'Saviour'; 'Redeemer'; 'King'.

A prayer can be shaped by taking a phrase such as 'O Thou who art the Way, the Truth and the Life' and expanding each idea separately:

'O Thou who art the Way ....

O Thou who art the Truth ....

O Thou who art the Life .... '

The choice of addressing God as 'thou' or 'you' is a personal one – but be consistent!

The following list contains only some of the possibilities. Others can be found in the Bible, particularly in the Psalms, or in hymns. The list is for you to choose from or adapt as suits your needs, in the confidence that God is ever more ready to listen than we are to approach him.

God the Father

– Almighty and everlasting God
– Dear Father God
– Eternal Father, strong to save
– Father of peace and God of love
– God of grace and God of glory
– Judge eternal, throned in splendour
– Lord of all being, throned afar
– Lord of beauty
– Lord of grace and truth
– Loving God, who guides us like a father
    and cares for us like a mother
– Merciful God, who knows our hidden thoughts
– O God, our loving heavenly father
– O God, our refuge and our strength
– O God, the giver of all good gifts
– O God, whose Word is a light to our pathway

God the Son

– Blessed Saviour
– Divine Teacher
– Eternal, living, loving Lord
– Jesus Christ, our Lord and King
– Jesus, good above all other
– Jesus, Master, whose we are and whom we serve
– Lamb of God
– Lord of all hope and all joy
– Lord, our light and our salvation
– Loving Shepherd
– Saviour of the World

God the Holy Spirit

– Gracious Spirit
– Holy Spirit, truth divine
– Life-giving Spirit, Comforter
– Love divine
– Spirit of love indestructible
– Spirit of peace
– Spirit of mercy, truth and love

PRAYERS
... of Adoration

Almighty and ever living God, we worship you –
Who set the stars in space –
    and designed primroses for a mossy bank.
You inhabit glory unimaginable –
    and yet you desire to live in our hearts.
We respond with love and praise –
You alone are worthy to be worshipped – honoured – adored.
We worship you.

*   *   *

As we gather for worship and fellowship,
to refresh our souls and to sit awhile at your feet,
Lord Jesus be our unity this night.
Take pleasure from all you experience of our love and faith,
shared with each other, for your sake.

*   *   *

Dear Loving Father,
We praise and worship you for you are a great and loving God.
We thank you for sending us your son, Jesus Christ,
to show us that love and to help us to see how you want us
to share that love with all around us.

Lord God, we cannot begin to understand
    how wonderful you are.
You have not only shown us a way of life
– YOU are the way! –
the way to God, the way to one another and the way of life.
You are the giver of life – life abundant,
life in the spirit and life eternal.
How can we praise you enough?
Made in your image, loved eternally and redeemed,
we praise you for the Holy Spirit to encourage us,
strengthen us, guide us, and comfort us.
Like Mary we can say,
'My soul is glad because of God my saviour,
for he has remembered me, his lowly servant.'
We worship, praise and adore you.

Lord, we praise you.
You are great and glorious.
You have shown your love,
your mercy toward us
in Jesus.
Lord we worship, we adore you.
In Jesus' name.

... of Confession

Heavenly Father, we come before you in Jesus' name,
confessing that
  in our actions and re-actions we have failed you,
  in our loving and forgiving we have fallen short of your
    mark,
  in our believing and trusting we have denied your grace
    and power.
In silence we lay before you the specific sins
which are clouding our relationship with you just now ....
We believe if we confess our sins
you will forgive and cleanse us.
Thank you for that;
so may we live as those who know we are forgiven
because of what Jesus has done for our lives.

* * *

Father,
Help us to confess our sin;
grant us the courage to examine ourselves candidly.
Bring to mind the thoughts, words and deeds of this day,
which have caused your Son to flinch with pain.   (*pause*)
Make us aware of any falseness in us.   (*pause*)
Help us to uncover the hidden motives which drive us,
and to recognise the distorted images we have of your love.
     (*pause*)

Have mercy on us; we are weak,
often misunderstanding and failing to listen to your Spirit
within.
We confess all this, and our great need of your love.
Confident in your commitment to us, we gladly share our
frailty with you,
our Redeemer, our Refuge and our Strength.

* * *

Almighty God, Father of us all, you are always with us and we can only ask your forgiveness for the many times we forget this in our daily lives. We bring all our burdens to you, Lord, our faults and hang-ups, our doubts and fears.

Lord, you know us – better than we know ourselves. You know our needs – and the greatest is you – to know true peace of mind and soul and that we are yours. Forgive us for the times we feel our faith is weak and we're just a 'dead loss'! But you are a God of mercy and you can change us.

Help us to see things with your eyes, to speak with your lips and to love with our Saviour's heart.

We depend on your mercy and trust in your love to overcome all that is evil without and within.

* * *

Forgive us that at times we don't love and care for others as we should; and help us to be more like our Saviour.

* * *

Loving Lord,
We ask forgiveness for the shallowness of caring.
We say we care,
yet we dodge the challenging issues that confront us,
as women, as Christians.
Our reasons and excuses come readily and sound so reason-
    able to us.
Forgive our closed minds, our fearfulness, our lack of spirit.
Help us to look squarely at the challenges, at the things that
    worry us and cause us to be fearful.
Afraid even to try lest we fail,
Afraid really to trust you.
Forgive us, Lord, for Jesus' sake.

... of Thanksgiving

Heavenly Father,
We thank you for our Branch/Group.
We thank you for the things that link us:
For shared worship,
Fellowship in prayer,
Opportunities to read and study the Bible,
The forging of bonds of friendship,
Ways to express together
a caring loving spirit in our congregation,
our home and community,
That all can see 'Whose we are and Whom we serve'!
Accept our love and thanks,
In the Saviour's name.

* * *

Almighty God,
We thank you for all we see of your own beauty
in the world you have created,
and in people's lives you are re-creating day by day.
We thank you for the details of love which enrich our lives
even when the going is difficult,
and we thank you most particularly for your love to us
in Jesus Christ who gives us purpose and hope today,
and for the future.
Thank you Lord.

* * *

Thank you Lord for our warm homes, our food, clothes and
all our comforts.
Thank you for family and friends who care about us.
Thank you that .... is out of hospital now.
Thank you that each one of us really matters to you.

* * *

Our loving and heavenly Father, you have given us everything
we have and all that we need. We thank you for your word the
Bible and we worship and adore the Christ whom we see in
its pages. We thank you for your faithfulness and your long-
suffering patience with us. We thank you for the gift of the
Holy Spirit, but most of all, dear Father, we thank you for your
greatest gift, your Son who is our Saviour, guide and friend
for ever – and to him be all the glory.

* * *

Thank you, Jesus, for knowing the secrets of our hearts –
the hopes, the fears, the joys, the doubts.
Thank you for experiencing all of these, as we do,
and for embracing them and us with compassion and courage,
and with the cross.

* * *

We thank you for the joy of being together and for the privilege
of being involved in the work of your church.

... for Others
and Ourselves

Gracious heavenly Father,
We pray for
– those who feel they have no need of you
– those whose suffering and sorrow are too great for us to share
– those who wait and pray in patience
– those who agonise over injustice
– those who show mercy and compassion
– those whose purity and grace inspire others
– those who work for peace where no peace seems possible
– those whose witness to truth and justice has brought them suffering.

Lord, teach us to pray with love and understanding;
to try to enter into the real needs that are around us;
to believe that through our prayers, you can heal and bless.
Through Jesus Christ, our Saviour and Lord.

* * *

Bless those of your children who have been called to serve you in far-off places and who face dangers quite unknown to us. Father, may they know that you are always with them, and grant them wisdom to know how to deal with the problems facing them.

* * *

Creator God, you made this beautiful world in which we live. As we watch the changing patterns of nature, we marvel and wonder and say 'How great thou art'. Help us to be good stewards of all that you have entrusted to our care. Help us to be thoughtful in the way we use the resources of this earth that we may set a good example to our children.

* * *

We pray for the leaders of the Sunday School and other youth organisations. We want our children to learn of your love and we ask you to bless all those who are giving their time to our young people. Sometimes they will be disheartened, but keep us faithful in praying and supporting them in every possible way. May they have the joy of seeing the children coming to know and love you.

* * *

We ask your blessing on our members, but especially we pray for those who are sick and housebound. Grant that we may not forget them, and show us ways of sharing with them the fellowship we will enjoy tonight. Be very near to any of our number who are facing anxiety and heartache and who feel they cannot cope. Loving Father, uphold them and grant them your strength and peace.

* * *

We pray for the young families in our midst. The pressures upon them are so great. Help them to know that you care for them and help them to know how to deal with all the demands placed upon them.

* * *

We bring to you our minister and his/her family. We thank you for them and for all they do for us. Bless them and help us to encourage them in their work for you.

*   *   *

O God, you are the strength of the weak, the refuge of the distressed, the comforter of the sad and the lover of our souls. In the name of Jesus we come asking you to help all those in need … the homeless, the victims of violence both domestic and global, those scarred by the wounds that life has inflicted upon them, the lonely and depressed; our ministers, missionaries and office bearers in the Guild …. We bring them all to you in faith, trusting in your love and mercy. We pray this in the name above all names, the Lord Jesus Christ.

*   *   *

We thank you
for all those people who work for you
in the various homes and hostels run by our church.
For those who seek to care for drug addicts
or those addicted to drink
and for whom life seems not to be worth living as it is.
Bless the work and witness of your children
and grant that your strength may be a reality
to those who seek to kick the habits which bind them.

Save us from being judgmental, but fill our hearts with loving understanding and a desire to help as and when we can.

Encourage the staff of these caring institutions – their disappointments are so hard to bear, but help them to stay close to you that your peace may always be theirs.

* * *

Father we remember before you the needs of others:
    those who feel rejected and unloved and unwanted,
    those who are terminally ill,
    those who are angry at the way they have been let down
      – who feel life is passing them by,
    those who have been made redundant
      but who would dearly love to have a job,
    those who are heartbroken
      because of the death of a dear loved one
– comfort them in their grief O Lord.

* * *

Father we pray for
    those who live in fear of any kind
      – help them to know you are with them,
    those who have to face prejudice
      because of their race and colour and tongue,
    those who are fearful of the future
      with all its uncertainties,
    those who face difficult decisions
      where there is no easy answer.

* * *

Let us pray for those who carry great stress
    because of family situations,
    those setting out on a new life together,
    those struggling to bring up a family
      without sufficient means to do so,
    those concerned for children who have left home
      and who don't know where they are

or what is happening to them,
those coping with a new home or new job or new baby,
those about to begin retirement,
those who have served your church over many years
    but who now feel out of things
    because they can no longer be actively involved.

*   *   *

Heavenly Father, we pray together for a world gone wrong, disturbed, unsettled.

Forgive us our part in that; invade us with your grace that through our love and care and sacrifice you might be more fully known in our community.

We pray for those who are ill,
    or worried about someone they love;   (*pause to reflect*)
We pray for homes where relationships
    are under real pressure;   (*pause to reflect*)
We pray for those facing decisions and new challenges;
                         (*pause to reflect*)
We pray for those who have lost heart and hope.
                         (*pause to reflect*)

Lord in your mercy hear our prayers
and touch these situations with your grace and love.
As we pray in Jesus' name.

Offering Prayers

Heavenly Father, you have given us riches beyond measure. We can only return a fraction of what we owe you; but we ask, Lord, that you will bless our offerings and help us to use them wisely in your service and for your glory.

* * *

What we give, we give freely.
What we have to give, we receive from your hands.
What we hold forever is your love for the world,
and for each of us.

* * *

Lord who loves a cheerful giver, accept these gifts of our heart given with joy; may they be a multiplied blessing in your service.

* * *

Lord, we don't know why we have so many of this world's benefits while others have nothing. We are filled with gratitude for the generosity you have shown to us. Accept our gifts, given in love. Bless them that they may bring hope and benefit to those in need. For the sake of Jesus.

* * *

'We give thee but thine own, whate'er the gift may be.'

Lord, so often we sing these words, yet fail to understand that all we have and all we are is due to your loving-kindness toward us. We thank you, Father, for family and friends, for fellowship and fun, for every opportunity to serve you and for all that makes our lives meaningful.

We ask you to accept our offerings which are but a small token of our gratitude and love for you, Lord. Bless them and use them to further your work throughout the world.

Through Jesus Christ we offer our prayer.

* * *

We bring these with our love, and ask that both them and us may be used for your glory.

Closing Prayers

We thank you Lord for being with us in this meeting, and thank you for the assurance that you will continue with each one of us as we go our separate ways.

* * *

Dear Father,
We thank you for your blessing on our meeting today. It has been good for us to leave aside the duties of the day to share this time of fellowship. Keep us aware of all that we have learned here and help us to do what we can to show your love through the lives we live.

Be with us as we go our separate ways. You know, dear Lord, the situations and demands to which we return. Grant to each one of us your strength to enable us to cope with whatever is asked and expected of us, that in all things we may know your loving presence to uphold us.

In Jesus' name we ask our prayer.

* * *

30

Lord, you have said, 'Wherever two or three are gathered together in my name – I am there'.

We praise and thank you for your presence here and for the
opportunity of meeting – may our fellowship have strengthened each one of us in our faith. Help us to love you as you
first loved us – and in loving you, help us to love our neighbours. May we be ready to serve you in our homes, in our
community and in your church.

We ask your blessing on the people we love and the homes we
return to, in Jesus' name.

* * *

Gracious heavenly Father,
Our time together has brought joy and a renewed awareness
of what our fellowship in Christ means. We have been uplifted,
challenged (comforted *etc*) and we thank you. We go from here
strengthened in our resolve to serve you.

May we know the presence of the Holy Spirit in our day to day
experience as we have done in our meeting tonight.
Bless our homes and families and keep us in your love always.
Through Jesus, our Lord.

* * *

Lord Jesus Christ, as we have shared in fellowship and worship here, may we go to our home situations and wider respon-
sibilities with a renewed sense of your presence and purposes.

31

Help us build into our lives the things we have heard about and considered today, that we will truly be a community of living faith which draws others to know you too.

*   *   *

Be with us in the quietness which follows company.
Speak to us as we reflect on this day closing.
Whisper our names in the silence before sleep.
Remain with us Lord, this night and always.

Benedictions

Heavenly Father – you have created us to love you.
Lord Jesus Christ – you came to show us that love.
Holy Spirit – fill each of us with the peace and joy
that comes from knowing that love.

* * *

Almighty God, we seek your blessing on each person here,
in our hearts and in our homes, for Jesus' sake.

* * *

Adapted from the Bible:

Now unto him that is able to keep us from falling, and to present
us faultless before the presence of his glory with exceeding
joy, to the only wise God our Saviour, be glory and majesty,
dominion and power, both now and ever.

Amen.

~ Jude 24 - 25 (AV) ~

May the Lord himself, who is our source of peace, give us
peace at all times and in every way. The Lord be with us all.

~ 2 Thessalonians 3: 16 (GNB) ~

The grace of the Lord Jesus Christ, the love of God, and the fellowship of the Holy Spirit be with us all.

~ 2 Corinthians 13:13 (GNB) ~

May the God of peace provide us with every good thing we need in order to do his will, and may he, through Jesus Christ, do in us what pleases him. And to Christ be the glory for ever and ever!

Amen.

~ Hebrews 13: 20 - 21 (GNB) ~

... at the Beginning
of a New Session

Almighty God,
Creator of all things and giver of all life,
We acknowledge your greatness and majesty
as we marvel at the works of your hand.

Thank you for all the happy times we have had since last we met
– for the times of rest and relaxation
– for the long summer days
and for the joy of being able to be out of doors.

We are glad to be together again Lord
as we look forward to the new session.
It's good for us to be here
to share the warmth of your love to each one of us.

Be with those who are with us for the first time – help us to make
them welcome and wanted, that they may know that they are
part of this family of the Woman's Guild.

Bless those of our number who are no longer able to be with
us. Let them know we are thinking of them tonight and keep us
ever aware of their need to know what we are doing. We ask
for a special blessing on the work of our visiting committee
throughout the coming months and may we all be willing to
help in this field of service.

Keep us ever mindful of our Aim and grant that during the weeks ahead we may do all we can to further the work of Christ throughout the world.

These prayers we ask through Jesus Christ,
our Saviour and Lord.

... for the Guild

Heavenly Father, we come to you today with things on our minds, from our families, from our work. Help us to lay them down and find your perspective and space. We seek together a new way of doing things. We thank you for all that makes life rich and full for us, for the new life made possible for us in Jesus Christ.

We pray for our country: that Christian values will determine our actions and be the inspiration for our leaders. Help us to be agents of healing where there is division in relationships or in communities. We pray for people in our communities whose lives are empty. Help us to be channels of your love and compassion.

Help us to know that we are part of your great design for the world and help us not to lose sight of the fact that each day you have some special task for us to do, which helps bring nearer God's kingdom here on earth.

We pray for your blessing on the Woman's Guild. Show us what road we are meant to take so that your message comes alive for so many more people. We thank you for those who have gone before us, for the heritage of the Guild and for the obedience and service of so many lives. Help us to be your disciples for our day and age. We rejoice to be part of your plan for the world and ask you to make us fit instruments for the carrying out of your will.

You are the light of the world; make us shine with Christ's love in our lives and let a light shine forth from our fellowship. Help us to take the quiet moments with you and let your peace run through our lives.

We commit our lives to your service.
For Jesus' sake.

Classic Prayers

Each thing I have received, from thee it came,
Each thing for which I hope, from thy love it will come,
Each thing I enjoy, it is of thy bounty,
Each thing I ask, comes of thy disposing.

~ Author unknown ~

* * *

I weave a silence to my lips ....
                    my mind ....
                    my heart ....

Calm me, O Lord,
as you stilled the storm.
Still me, O Lord,
keep me from harm.
Let all the tumult within me cease.
Enfold me, Lord,
In your peace.

~ David Adam[3] ~

* * *

O God,
as truly as you are our Father,
so just as truly you are our Mother.
We thank you, God our Father,
for your strength and goodness.
We thank you, God our Mother,
for the closeness of your caring.
O God, we thank you for the
great love you have for
each one of us.

~ Mother Julian of Norwich (14th century)[4] ~

* * *

Take, Lord
and receive all my liberty,
my memory, my understanding
and my entire will,
all that I have and possess.

You have given all to me;
to you, Lord, I return it.

All is yours;
do with it what you will.

Give me only your love
and your grace;
that is enough for me.

~ St Ignatius Loyola[5] ~

Favourite Prayers

Be Still

Time for myself ....Why is it that I find it so hard to take time for myself? Time to be, rather than to do. Time to think, to talk to God, and most of all to be silent in his presence while he talks to me.

You know how it is Lord! There is always so much to be fitted in. People to be seen ... work to be done ... obligations to fulfil. It is so difficult to distinguish between the urgent and the important. Often what is urgent elbows its way to the forefront of my day and the important gets trampled on in the rush.

Slow me down, Lord. Teach me the art of creating islands of stillness, in which I can absorb the beauty of everyday things: clouds, trees, a snatch of music. Prompt me to lift up my heart to you in a moment of thankfulness. Impress upon my mind that there is more to life than packing every moment with activity, and help me to fence in some part of my day with quietness. And please talk to me and help me to listen, so that I take your peace rather than my confusion back with me into the hurly-burly of a hurting world.

~ Marion Stroud, *The Gift of Friends* (Lion Publishing) ~

* * *

Take me, Lord, from busyness
to the place of quietness,
From the tumult without cease,
into your great unending peace,
Help me then, my Lord,
to see what I am and ought to be.

~ David Adam[6] ~

* * *

Tourist's Prayer

O Lord, I don't want to be a spectator
A tour passenger looking out upon the real world
An audience to poverty and want and homelessness.
Lord, involve me – call me
And Lord – help me to step off the bus.

~ Freda Rajotte[7] ~

* * *

Lord God, you created all equal,
All in your image and likeness.
Help us to work to remove the injustices
Which lead to some being more equal than others.
May our hands be your hands,
To bring relief to the poor, the hungry, the needy.
May our ears be your ears,
To hear the groans of the oppressed.
May our healing be your healing,
To give food to the hungry, hope in despair.
To bring freedom to captives and all those enslaved.
May we, in partnership with all creation, work together
To bring about God's Kingdom of Justice and Peace.

~ SCIAF[8] ~

... from around
the World

Russia

Too long have I worried about so many things;
And yet, my Lord, so few are needed!
May I, today, live more simply
 – like the bread:
May I, today, see more clearly
 – like the water:
May I, today, be more selfless
 – like the Christ

The Philippines

Lord, in these times,
when we feel we are losing hope,
or feel our efforts are futile,
let us see in our hearts and minds
the image of your resurrection,
and let that be our source of courage and strength.
With that, and in your company,
help us to face challenges and struggles
against all that is born of injustice.

Chile

Empower me, Lord,
to take the risks of faith today
for your sake and the gospel.

South Africa

Father and Friend
help us to learn
that goodness is stronger than evil;
that love is stronger than hate;
that light is stronger than darkness;
that life is stronger than death;
and that every victory is ours
through your forgiving love.

~ Bishop Desmond Tutu ~

Paraphrase and Prayer
based on 1 Corinthians 13

I may be able to communicate well and express sublime and heavenly truths, but if I have no deep concern in my heart, I shall provoke no better response than if I blew on a trumpet or banged on a gong.

I may be clever enough to know all there is to know, and even be able to tell accurately what is going to happen in the future. I may have such complete faith in God that nothing is impossible to me, but unless I love God above all else, I shall amount to nothing.

If I were to give everything I have to feed the hungry, and were even to sacrifice my life for others, unless I truly cared for those people, I should achieve precisely nothing.

LOVE is like this:

It is very patient.
It tries to build people up.
It is always kind to them, in thought, speech and action.

Love is never jealous of others.
It doesn't keep trying to impress upon other people
    how important it is.

Love is never rude.
It displays good manners at all times
 and never puts itself first.
Love does not become irritable or touchy,
 nor does it grow resentful.
Love doesn't keep dwelling on the faults of others,
 or pride itself on its own goodness by comparison.
It doesn't rub its hands and chuckle with glee
 when others go wrong.
On the contrary, it is delighted and full of thankfulness,
 along with all good people,
 when goodness, justice and truth come out on top.

LOVE has superhuman endurance.
It goes right on believing in the best,
 never losing its hope
 that God will have his way with the world.

LOVE cannot be beaten, it never dies, it will not fail.

Let us pray:

Father,
we thank you that by so many means
 you show your love for us.
You give us the world in which we live,
you make us part of a family and members of a community
 in which we find our friends.
You show yourself to us in Jesus,
 whose love for us took him to the cross.

We thank you that we learn from you
    that love is the key to life.
Without it all our activity is worthless.
With love, even that which looks like failure and defeat
    can be used to create something new
    or build up something old.

Forgive us
    for being so unlike Jesus,
    for losing patience with each other,
    for trying to break each other down with our criticisms
    and lack of understanding.

Forgive us
    for trying to impress others with our own ideas of ourselves,
    for using others to raise our own self-respect,
    for blaming them when our relationships are unsatisfactory.

Forgive us
    for our unkindness towards each other,
    especially for what we sometimes say about people
    behind their backs.

Forgive us
    for our jealousy of one another
    and for the spitefulness that sometimes goes with it.

Forgive us
    for being quick to take offence
    and for becoming resentful when others get the praise
    and our work goes unnoticed and unrewarded.

Forgive us
　　when we take pleasure in other people's faults or mistakes,
　　and when we brood over wrongs done to us
　　so that they sour all our relationships.

Help us to forgive others
　　so that we may receive your forgiveness.

Lord, we thank you that your love for us is our salvation. Where should we be without your love? Only love like yours can bend down and rescue us. Only love like yours can forgive us and make us whole.

Thank you for your saving work in us
through the love of Jesus Christ our Lord.　　　　　　*Amen.*

An Outline Prayer

A particularly simple, yet effective outline for prayer can be devised by using the outline of 'Kum ba yah' ... 'Come by here'.

Use the opening line of each verse, not necessarily in the printed order, for that can depend on the meeting, and the content can be varied to cover many items of concern. The appropriate verse of 'Kum ba yah' could be sung in between each section of the prayer, if desired.

Let us pray:

Kum ba yah, Lord ... come by here ... and let us know your presence in our hearts, in our minds, in our thoughts, tonight.

As we listen to your word, sing your praise, bring our prayers to you, make us aware of your Holy Spirit within us, leading us and guiding us to a deeper faith.

Come by here, Lord.

Someone's crying, Lord ...

We remember before you those who are ill ... comfort and uphold them in the warmth of your love. Give them courage in their pain, and hope of relief from their discomfort.

Grant strength and patience to those who bear the responsibility of caring for the sick, in body or mind.

We pray for those who are anxious for loved ones, support
them in their concern, and lead them to an awareness of your
sustaining love.

Come by here, Lord.

We pray for those whose lives are disrupted by war, or natural
disaster ... for the starving, the refugee, the homeless. May
leaders of war-torn countries learn tolerance and understanding, that peace may ensue. Let reason prevail, that all may
love their neighbour, however different. Preserve the safety of
those whose aid is a life-line to the victims.

Come by here, Lord.

Someone's praying, Lord ... and we would pray for those
who use their skills to further your work. For our speaker this
evening ... we ask a special blessing.

We pray for all Guildswomen ... for our Office-bearers and
our committee members. For the work, local and national
attempted in your name, by our organisation.

Come by here, Lord.

Someone's singing, Lord ... and we praise you for all your
goodness to us. We recognise you in the green buds and in the

bright flowers peeping through the soil, and in the fine spring days, all reassuring us of your promise of new life. We pray that we will be careful custodians of your great creation, that our children will inherit an unpolluted earth, and also know your benefits. Most of all Lord, we praise you for that greatest gift ... your Son, our Saviour, Jesus Christ, who did indeed 'Come by here', teaching us to pray together, saying –

Our Father, who art in heaven ....

ANOTHER WAY TO PRAY
Contemplation of the Gospels

Increasingly an interest is being shown in a very ancient method of prayer: imaginative contemplation of the Gospels.

What is it and could it be fruitful for our members?

Contemplation (or meditation as it is sometimes called) seeks to use the memory and imagination to flesh out a story from the Gospel. We all have a storehouse of memories: experiences, feelings, moods, sights, sounds, smells *etc*. We know that a smell can evoke a memory which we re-live in our imaginations and enjoy again. A song may recall a painful memory and we actually feel the pain of the situation again.

Psychology confirms that value and power of our memory and imagination for the health of a whole person. Contemplation of the Gospels accepts both as gifts of God for our spiritual health.

When we contemplate we imagine the scene – *eg* the two disciples walking to Emmaus – and with the help of our own memories of walks we have taken (smells, noises, sights and feelings) we enter into the picture with the characters, perhaps even taking the part of one of them in our imagination.

What is the object of contemplation?

Christians believe that the Word of God is alive and active. By the use of our imagination we allow Scripture to speak to us in a personal way, through our own experienced sensations and feelings. When a person says: *'That Bible reading just spoke to me today',* it probably did so because a chord was struck in the listener's memory. Much comfort can be found through contemplation. Also, since God always seeks to draw us closer to him, contemplation can disturb us, as we discover new aspects of his call on our lives.

Are there any dangers?

Only that your members will not enjoy this method of prayer. God loves variety, and contemplation is simply one of many ways to enter his presence and listen for his voice.

There is no hypnotism whatsoever involved and each member can choose to stay with the imagined scene for as long as she is comfortable. Some may be so comfortable that there is a danger they will drop off to sleep!

To find out more about this method read:

- Foster: *Celebration of Discipline*
- Huggett: *Listening to God*
- Hughes: *God of Surprises*

What do we need, to begin?

A space of fifteen minutes in the worship programme. A person willing to lead, by reading the passage slowly and clearly, and then by inviting the members to picture the scene, become aware of the people, the scenery or setting, the noises, colours *etc.* This person has to give the members time to relax into their imagination, but can also offer help by occasionally and quietly asking a question. For example:

'Are you present in the scene?' – 'Who are you?'

'What can you hear?' 'What feelings are you aware of?'

'What do you want to tell Jesus?'
'What does Jesus say to you?'

The questions must be open enough to be helpful to everyone, and may differ according to the passage being used.

An introductory exercise which uses the memory and imagination in a way with which we are all familiar may be a useful starting point. Try the one below. A relaxation exercise or a piece of music can help people to still themselves in preparation; this need not be long and could lead straight into the contemplation. The chosen leader may wish to tape the reading and the guiding questions, leaving spaces of two minutes or so between each one and simply play the tape at the meeting. As confidence grows the 'live' delivery will be preferred as this allows for the Spirit to suggest quietly a good guiding question. A couple of friends might volunteer to listen and 'do' the contemplation.

Introductory Exercise
in Contemplation

I invite you to recall to mind a happy memory – a place, a time, an event which was for you one of great joy. I will ask you to re-play the memory as though you are watching a video.

Don't worry if you find yourself becoming distracted. Simply go through the relaxation exercise again (if appropriate) and replace that distraction with the memory you have recalled.

Now, if you can, bring a happy memory to mind and enjoy the scene in your imagination.

    (*pause*)

    What can you see?

    What can you hear?

    What can you smell?

    (*pause*)

    Are you aware of colours, music, voices, faces?

    Enjoy this scene from your life for a little while.

(pause)

Now I would like you to leave the scene for a moment and become aware of *this* moment in time, this room, keeping your eyes closed.

What sounds are you aware of inside the room?
And outside?

What are you feeling?

Are you aware of any feelings of peace, joy, excitement spilling over from your special memory into this moment?

Go back once more to that special memory and savour the experience.

(pause)

This memory holds much encouragement and strength for you. Hear the words spoken to you or experience again the sensations which make this memory a happy one.

Enjoy the people there, or the colours, the smells, the scenery.

Enjoy the positive way you feel about yourself.

(pause)

Now return again to this moment in time, but try to bring with you some of those positive feelings.

Be aware of this room, the noises, smells, the chair upon which you sit.

What feelings are you aware of in yourself?

Perhaps you can express gratitude for the enjoyment of your memory, giving thanks for the people, the places which have brought happiness in the past and which can still be a source of strength and joy in your life.

As you do this enjoy a piece of music and allow the good feelings to soar in your heart.

Contemplation
of a Gospel Passage

John 20: 19 - 21

A SIMPLE RELAXATION EXERCISE AS BEFORE
WOULD BE USEFUL.

> I am going to read a short passage from the gospel. I will read
> it through twice.

> Try to picture the scene described, laying aside any intel-
> lectual questions about the passage for the moment.

> In the evening of that same day, the first day of the week, the
> doors were closed in the room where the disciples were, for
> fear of the Jews. Jesus came and stood among them. He said
> to them, 'Peace be with you', and showed them his hands and
> his side. The disciples were filled with joy when they saw the
> Lord, and he said to them again, 'Peace be with you. As the
> Father sent me, so I am sending you'.

> *~ Jerusalem Bible ~*

READ THE PASSAGE SLOWLY AGAIN.

THEN, AFTER A PAUSE, SAY:

> Try to imagine the scene, but do not worry if you became

distracted, simply replace the distracting thought with the phrase 'Peace be with you', saying it over as you breathe out.

(*pause*)

As you imagine the scene, can you see the room, expressions on faces, hear voices?

Perhaps you could imagine yourself present in the room, talking with the men and women.

(*pause*)

Christ appears. Feel the reaction of the group. What are you feeling?

Hear Christ speak to you.

What does his peace mean for you?

Stay with this scene for a few minutes and ask God to speak to you through it.

(*pause of a few minutes*)

We are going to leave this scene now. Listen to the music and let Christ's peace fill you.

PLAY SOME GENTLE MUSIC

AFTER THE TIME OF QUIET, PEOPLE MAY WANT TO
SHARE THEIR EXPERIENCE. SOME MAY NOT HAVE
BEEN COMFORTABLE AND NEED TO EXPRESS THIS.
OTHERS MAY WISH NOT TO SHARE.

BE SENSITIVE TO NEEDS.

The best way to discover is to do, and it is of course possible,
even preferable, to discover imaginative contemplation in private and personal devotions before attempting to lead a group
into it.

Other suitable Gospel passages include:

Mark	2: 1 - 12	Healing of the paralysed man
Mark	4: 35 - 41	Jesus calms the storm
Mark	10: 13 - 16	Jesus blesses the children
Luke	9: 10 - 17	Feeding of the five thousand
John	12: 1 - 8	Mary anoints Jesus

Meditation
on Violence

(This meditation might be particularly suitable for the end of a meeting, for example, when the subject has been the work of Amnesty International or Women's Aid):

Be still and know God:
Be still and know that he will heal you:
Be still and put your trust in the Lord.

Violence has many shades. Everyone has been the victim of violence in one form or another and we are all guilty of violence in word or thought, if not in deed.

Take some time to read Matthew 27: 15 - 26. As you read, imagine that you are one of the disciples or one of the crowd.

Did you shout for Barabbas? Did you deny Jesus? How do you feel?

Violence is often dressed up in religious clothes, as in Northern Ireland today or in Egypt three thousand years ago. Each side tells us they are justified in killing; what we must remember is that God doesn't take sides. God loved the Egyptians and Israelites alike and he made no distinction between Jew and Greek. God doesn't have favourites; so why then, does he allow violence? Why is violence all around us – in war, in street crime and in our own homes where there should be love and trust and security?

The answer is that God does not allow these things. He does, however, allow us the privilege of freedom and choice. If we stray too far from him, then we are responsible for making the wrong choices.

If we are hurting, God is there for us; all we have to do is ask. Ask for comfort, for help, for strength, especially the strength and the grace to forgive. Ask also, that God be with the afflictor, where help is vital.

Now read Matthew 5: 38 - 48:

Along with our feelings of betrayal, hurt, rejection and bitterness must come forgiveness. For without love and forgiveness we will not heal and cannot be whole again.

Be aware of those around you, be sensitive to their situation. God will enable you to hold out your arms for them and enfold them in the shelter of your love.

Prayer:

Loving Lord God,
Be our shelter and our strength, always ready to help in times of trouble. Help us to face the storms of life for they will often catch us unawares when our defences are down and our spirit is at a low ebb.

Lord, we ask that you enable us not to judge or apportion blame. Give us grace, Lord, to turn the other cheek. Heavenly Father, as you help us in all our troubles, we shall endeavour to hold out our arms to others in need, giving them the help we receive from you.

As we sail the ocean of storms, Father,
be Lord of our rocking boat. *Amen.*

Any of the following may be used in conjunction with the meditation if used in a group setting:

Hymns: SGP   19   Christ be beside me
            SGP   48   I need thee every hour
            CH3 669   Put thou thy Trust in God
            CH3 115   Come down O Love Divine

63

THE PSALMS
The Prayer Book of Jesus

Few of us will have escaped a time in our lives when our private prayer life has fallen to pieces. During such difficult times, using the Psalms as a base line for private prayer can give a stability to daily prayer not otherwise experienced.

Why is it that the Psalms prove so helpful? There are three main reasons for this:

First, *the Psalms were the very bedrock of the family and personal prayers of the Hebrew people and, therefore, of Jesus himself.* They were basic to the liturgy of his people, and Jesus, like so many others, would have prayed them so often that he knew them by heart. We find good evidence for this in the Bible. When Jesus was cornered and could scarcely, under the pain of the cross, find words with which to pray, he was able to summon a prayer from the Psalms to express his deepest anguish: 'My God, why … ?' (Psalm 22). It seems that Jesus handled the pain of the crucifixion by praying. According to St Luke, Jesus died praying. His very last words before his death were a prayer which he had learned, night after night, at his mother's knee: 'Into your hands I commit my spirit' (Psalm 31).

The Psalter was clearly Jesus' prayer book. He had, one might say, interiorised the Psalms – made them part of his very being

– and could, when scarcely able to articulate a prayer of his own, draw from the Psalms to offer to his Father his deepest feeling of anguish and commitment.

This is why the Psalms have been found by so many to be such a source of strength and comfort. As we pray them, we take into our minds and hearts the very prayers which Jesus prayed. Some believe, in fact, that Jesus still prays these Psalms of praise and that, in entering into them we may enter now into his life of praycr to his father.

The second reason why the Psalms have been found to be so helpful is a personal one and relates to how we-ourselves may be feeling as we set aside time to pray.

Sometimes we may be so tired that we cannot find words to pray. We cannot bring them to a rational focus or articulate them, and here in the Psalms they are given to us – as graciously given as everything else that God gives to us. *Words of praise are given and words of sorrow.*

Most of us come to our prayers, whenever, with conflicting moods. We might get up feeling full of joy in God, and can readily drop into a Psalm of praise. But then there follows a Psalm of sorrow, in which we are invited into a low time with the Psalmist, and to feel with him his anguish. Our own spirits cannot be allowed to forget that there are others in this world, the sick, the hungry, those without work, who are not feeling the joy which we feel that day, and if we are to live our lives with any kind of sensitivity, we must be helped to feel with them. This the Psalms of sorrow can do for us. We might, however, simply be feeling low, apprehensive about the tasks before us.

We find in the Psalmist one with a fellow-feeling. But the entrenched Psalm of praise can raise our hearts and does. So, God by his grace evens our spirits for living our lives with serenity.

The third reason why the Psalms are so helpful is that *the themes of the Psalms seem to embrace the whole of life*. Anyone praying the Psalms can make their own selection out of the wide expanse of life which the Psalms cover. The Psalmist gives thanks for the beauty of the natural order – 'The heavens declare the glory of God ... ' (Psalm 19). He prays about daily work and about the harvest – 'The soil has given its harvest. God has blessed us!' (Psalm 67). Psalms were written for the occasion of a marriage (Psalm 45) and celebrated the delighted shrieks of children (Psalm 8). They were also written for the down side of life when the Psalmist was suffering such anguish from disease and pain and such feeling of guilt that he felt his life was nearing its end (Psalm 38). At least one Psalm was written by a deportee out of the bitterness of ethnic cleansing and captivity. The Psalms have profound integrity because they deal with the gut issues of daily life.

There are many ways by which one may pray the Psalms. It is possible, for example, to pray the Psalms through from 1 to 150 following a twice yearly cycle. This simple pattern of prayer was devised by Annie Small, one of the founding mothers at St Colm's Centre and College, who was a person of profound spirituality, delighted in the Psalms (and, indeed, wrote a very beautiful book on them) and tried to find practical ways to help missionaries in training with their devotional lives. Her Psalm-cycle is included in a small booklet entitled *Traditions Which Endure*. Again, we may seek to deepen our understanding of the Psalms, as we pray them, by reading them with a commentary of some depth. Others will find yet other ways of their own to pray the Psalms.

The praying of the Psalms is an act of commitment to the renewal of the church. It is a simple fact that, whenever in the history of the church there has been dynamic growth, this has been accompanied by the rediscovery of the central importance of the Psalms as a medium by which we may worship God. The early church sang 'psalms, hymns and spiritual songs'. At the time of the Gregorian revival (AD 600) and in the monastic movement, the chanting of the Psalms in praise of God was the bedrock of liturgical prayer.

At the time of the Reformation, Christians in Scotland uncovered the Psalms in their own language for their own heartfelt praise of God and metricised them to enable them to be learned and sung by illiterate people. In our own day new translations of the Psalms with new modes of singing are unlocking them afresh for us. To pray the Psalms is to stand entirely in a tradition of prayer to God in which we enter deeply into the prayer of Jesus and his people and allow our own lives to be deepened and brightened for the praise of God and the service of his kingdom.

Praying
through the Psalms

Father, you know us as we are,
our faults and failures as well as our successes.

Lord, you have examined me and you know me.
You know everything I do;
From far away you understand all my thoughts.
You see me, whether I am working or resting;
You know all my actions.
Even before I speak, you already know what I will say.
You are all round me on every side;
You protect me with your power.
Your knowledge of me is too deep;
It is beyond my understanding.
Examine me, O God, and know my mind,
test me and discover my thoughts.
Find out if there is any evil in me
and guide me in the everlasting way.

~ Psalm 139 (GNB) ~

Adoration and praise are often far from our thoughts as we
rush through our daily life.

I thank you Lord, with all my heart;
I sing praise to you before the gods.

I face your holy Temple, bow down and praise your name
because of your constant love and faithfulness,
because you have shown that your name
and your commands are supreme.
You answered me when I called to you;
with your strength you strengthened me.
You will do everything you have promised;
Lord your love is eternal,
Complete the work that you have begun.

~ Psalm 138 (GNB) ~

Inspire us to greater heights of hope and depths of belief.

You have done many things for us, O Lord our God;
there is no-one like you!
You have made wonderful plans for us.
I could never speak of them all – their number is so great!
May all who come to you be glad and joyful.
May all who are thankful for your salvation
always say 'How great is the Lord'.

~ Psalm 40 (GNB) ~

Life is often hard, the decisions and compromises we make
can leave us unhappy with the choices we have made.

Be good to me, your servant,
so that I may live and obey your teachings.
Open my eyes,
so that I may see the wonderful truths in your law.
I am here on earth for just a little while;

do not hide your commands from me.
My heart aches with longing:
I want to know your judgments at all times.
Your instructions give me pleasure;
they are my advisers.

~ Psalm 119 (GNB) ~

Uphold us when we are troubled, when we are sinking in deep mud and there is no solid ground, when we are worn out calling for help.

Answer me Lord, in the goodness of your constant love;
in your compassion, turn to me!
Don't hide yourself from your servant;
I am in great trouble – answer me now!
Come to me and save me.

~ Psalm 69 (GNB) ~

Renew in us a calmness of spirit that we may hear your still small voice above the noise of our confusion.

The Lord Almighty is with us.
Come and see what the Lord has done.
See what amazing things he has done on earth.
He stops wars all over the world;
He breaks bows, destroys spears and sets shields on fire.
'Stop fighting,' he says, 'and know that I am God,
supreme among the nations, supreme over the world.'

~ Psalm 46 (GNB) ~

Everything we do, we would do to glorify your name, but how often we fall short of that goal.

To you alone, O Lord, and not to us, must glory be given because of your constant love and faithfulness.

~ Psalm 115 (GNB) ~

Hear our prayer, O Lord, and let our cry come unto you.

A GUIDE TO
BIBLE READINGS

From the Old Testament

A sign of hope	Genesis	9:	8 - 17
Abraham obeys God	Genesis	12:	1 - 9
The Ten Commandments	Exodus	20:	1 - 20
Where you go, I will go	Ruth	1:	1 - 22
Hannah's prayer	1 Samuel	1:	9 - 20
Elijah and the Widow	1 Kings	17:	8 - 24
A virtuous wife	Proverbs	31:	10 - 31
Confidence in God	Isaiah	40:	21 - 31
Rivers in the desert	Isaiah	43:	1 - 21
The promise of good things	Jeremiah	29:	10 - 14
A new covenant	Jeremiah	31:	31 - 34
Covenant of peace	Ezekiel	34:	25 - 31
Dry bones	Ezekiel	37:	1 - 10
Repentance and restoration	Hosea	14:	1 - 9
An age of peace	Micah	4:	1 - 7

From the Psalms

The heavens declare God's glory	Psalm	19	
The earth is the Lord's		24:	1 - 6
Trust in the Lord		37:	1 - 9
Prayer for forgiveness		51:	1 - 12

God blesses us	Psalm	67
Trust in God		91: 1 - 6
A new song		96
The Lord is God		100
Prayer for God's help		118: 1 - 6
Looking to the Lord		123
Out of the depths		130
O Lord, my heart is not proud		131
Confidence		138
Search me, O Lord		139: 1 - 18, 23 - 24
Universal praise		150

From the New Testament

Mary's Song of Praise	Luke	1: 46 - 55
Zechariah's Prophecy	Luke	1: 67 - 79
Song of Simeon	Luke	2: 25 - 35

Events in the life of Jesus

Baptism	Matthew	3: 13 - 17
Calling the disciples	Matthew	4: 18 - 22
Sending out the disciples	Mark	6: 7 - 13
Peter's declaration	Mark	8: 27 - 30
Transfiguration	Mark	9: 2 - 9
Entry into Jerusalem	Mark	11: 1 - 11
Anointment at Bethany	Mark	14: 3 - 9
Last Supper	Matthew	26: 26 - 30
Crucifixion	Luke	23: 26 - 49
Resurrection	Mark	16: 1 - 7
Walk to Emmaus	Luke	24: 13 - 35

Miracles

Calming the storm	Luke	8: 22 - 25
Feeding the five thousand	Mark	6: 35 - 44
Healing of the lepers	Luke	17: 11 - 19
Healing of the paralysed man	Mark	2: 1 - 12
Healing of Simon's mother	Mark	1: 29 - 34
Healing of the woman who touched his cloak	Luke	8: 43 - 48
Walking on water	John	6: 15 - 21

Teachings of Jesus

Ask, seek, knock	Matthew	7: 7 - 12
Beatitudes	Matthew	5: 1 - 12
Blessing the children	Mark	10: 13 - 16
Do not worry	Matthew	6: 25 - 34
Feed my sheep	John	21: 15 - 19
Greatest Commandment	Mark	12: 28 - 34
I am the way, the truth, and the life	John	14: 1 - 7
Judgment of the sheep and the goats	Matthew	25: 31 - 46
Life-giving water	John	4: 5 - 14
Love your enemies	Luke	6: 27 - 36
Parable of the Good Samaritan	Luke	10: 29 - 37
Parable of the Prodigal Son	Luke	15: 11 - 24
Parable of the Sower	Matthew	13: 3 - 9, 18 - 23
Prayer	Matthew	6: 5 - 15

The Early Church

Coming of the Holy Spirit	Acts	2: 1 - 4
Conversion of Saul	Acts	9: 1 - 9
Grace and faith	Romans	5: 1 - 11
If God is for us	Romans	8: 31 - 39
One Body	1 Corinthians	12: 12 - 27
Love	1 Corinthians	13
Armour of God	Ephesians	6: 10 - 18
Faith and actions	James	2: 14 - 24
God is Light	1 John	1: 5 - 9

SUGGESTIONS FOR
USING THE BIBLE

For our personal preparation before leading meetings:

The right attitude	Psalm 19: 7 - 14;
	Ephesians. 5: 1 - 2, 15 - 17
Seeking forgiveness	Psalm 51: 1, 2, 6 - 15;
	Luke 24: 45 - 47
The promise of God's help	Joshua 1: 1, 5 - 9;
	Matthew 28: 19 - 20
Thanksgiving	Psalm 103: 1 - 14;
	1 Thessalonians 5: 14 - 16

*Passages particularly suitable for reading
as part of worship:*

Who God is	Isaiah 40: 21 - 31; John 1: 1 - 5
God's promise	
to send the Messiah	Isaiah 42: 1 - 7; Luke 1: 26 - 38
The future of the nation	2 Chronicles 7: 12 - 20;
	Luke 22: 24 - 30
Coming to God	Psalm 100; Psalm 130
Walking with God	Isaiah 35
Security in God	Psalm 23; Psalm 121;
	John 10: 7 - 10;
	Romans 8: 31 - 39

Themes with related Readings and Hymns

Be Prepared	Matt.	25:	1 - 13	CH3 319	Ye servants of the Lord

* * *

Building the Church	1 Peter	2:	4 - 10	CH3 339 MP 50	O Breath of life For I'm building a people of power

* * *

Caring	Lev.	25:	35 - 43	MP 157	May the mind of Christ
	Gal.	6:	1 - 10	CH3 450	Saviour, teach me

* * *

Celebration	Ps.	96:	7 - 13	CH3 296	Rejoice, the Lord is King
	Luke.	15:	8 - 10	SGP 59	Jubilate, everybody

* * *

Choices	Deut.	30:	15 - 20	CH3 663	O for a closer walk with God
	Matt.	6: 24		SGP 48	I need thee every hour
	Luke	10:	38 - 42	SGP 93	Seek ye first

* * *

Christmas	Isa.	9:	2, 6, 7	CH3 172	O little town of Bethlehem
	Micah	5: 2		CH3 173	The first Nowell

	Matt.	1: 18 - 25	CH3 180	Child in the manger
		2: 1 - 12		
	Luke	2: 1 - 20	CH3 194	Love came down

* * *

Conservation	Gen.	1: 26 - 31	CH3 451	Almighty Father
			SGP 70	Lord bring the
				day to pass

* * *

Creator God	Gen.	1: 1 - 12	SGP 78	Morning has broken
	John	1: 1 - 5	SGP 86	O Lord my God
	Acts	17: 24 - 28	CH3 120	Lord of beauty

* * *

Differing gifts	1 Cor.	12: 12 - 31	CH3 455	Angel voices
			SGP 65	Let us talents

* * *

Faith	Matt.	8: 5 - 13	CH3 81	My faith looks
				up to thee
	Matt.	17: 14 - 21	CH3 664	O for a faith
	Hebs.	10: 22 - 25	SGP 107	Through the love
				of God
	Hebs.	12: 1 - 2	SGP 69	Look forward
				in faith
	James	2: 14 - 26	CH3 669	Put thou thy
				trust in God

* * *

Forgiveness	Matt.	18: 21 - 35	SGP 33	God forgave my sin
	Ephs.	4: 29 - 32	CH3 77	Father of heaven

	Cols.	3: 12 - 17	CH3 90	Lead us, heavenly Father
	1 John	1: 5 - 10	CH3 85	O for a heart

* * *

Good Friday	Isa.	53	CH3 259	In the cross of Christ I glory
	Mark	15	CH3 241	There is a green hill
	Luke	22: 66 - 71	CH3 254	When I survey
	Luke	23	SGP 114	Were you there

* * *

Good News	Mark	1: 1 - 8	SGP 45	How lovely on the mountains
	John	3: 16 - 21	CH3 130	Lord, thy word abideth
	Rom.	1: 16 - 17	CH3 475	We have heard a joyful sound

* * *

Grace	2 Cor.	12: 7 - 10	SGP 9	Amazing grace
	Ephs.	1: 3 - 8	CH3 94	O Jesus strong and pure and true
	Ephs.	2: 4 - 10	CH3 216	What grace, O Lord

* * *

Holy Land	Ps.	122	CH3 4	How lovely is thy dwelling place
	Luke	19: 37 - 44	CH3 312	Behold the mount-tain of the Lord

79

* * *

Holy Spirit	Ezek.	36: 23 - 28	CH3 104	Come, Holy Spirit, come
	John	14: 15 - 20	CH3 11	Jesus, stand among us
	Acts	1: 6 - 11	SGP 4	All over the world
	Gal.	5: 16 - 23	CH3 106	Holy Spirit, Truth Divine

* * *

Hope	Rom.	5: 1 - 5	CH3 396	Behold the amazing gift of love
	1 Cor.	15: 12 - 20	CH3 92	Lord of all hopefulness
	2 Cor.	3: 12 - 18	SGP 107	Through the love of God

* * *

Joy	Luke	15: 1 - 10	CH3 366	Sing to the Lord a joyful song
	John	15: 1 - 11	CH3 111	Jesus, good above all other
	Rom.	15: 10 - 13	SGP 120	You shall go out with joy
	Phil.	1: 3 - 11	CH3 296	Rejoice the Lord is King

* * *

| Justice | Lev. | 19: 11 - 18 | CH3 323 | Thy kingdom come |

* * *

Keeping	Lev.	19: 1 - 2	SGP 105	This is the day
Sunday	Isa.	58: 13 - 14	MP 97	I will enter his
Special				gates
	Jer.	17: 19 - 27	CH3 76	Dear Lord
				and Father

* * *

Leadership	Acts	20: 28 - 35	CH3 510	Lord of light
			SGP 34	Go, tell everyone

* * *

Light	John	1: 1 - 7	CH3 32	Immortal, invisible
	John	3: 18 - 21	CH3 34	Lord of all being
	Ephs.	5: 6 - 14	MP 714	Lord, the light of
				your love is shining
	1 John	1: 5 - 7	SGP 102	The spirit lives
	Rev.	22: 1 - 5	CH3 53	Before the day draws
				near its ending

* * *

Love	John	13: 31 - 35	SGP 2	A new
				commandment
	Rom.	8: 31 - 39	CH3 437	Love divine
	Ephs.	3: 14 - 21	MP 11	And can it be
	Phil.	2: 2 - 11	CH3 218	There's a wideness
				in God's mercy
	1 John	4: 7 - 21	CH3 144	God is love

* * *

Mental Health	1 Kgs	19: 4 - 12	SGP 24	Do not be afraid
	Luke	4: 33 - 37	CH3 52	At even when the
				sun was set

* * *

Mission	Isa.	40: 1 - 11	CH3 164	Tell out my soul
	Isa.	43: 8 - 13	MP 261	We've a story to tell
	Mal.	3: 1, 16 - 18	SGP 4	All over the world
	Matt.	28: 18 - 20	SGP 34	Go, tell everyone
	Acts	1: 1 - 14	SGP 33	God forgave my sin
	2 Cor.	5: 14 - 21	CH3 463	Forth in thy Name

* * *

Neglect by parents	Ps.	27: 1, 7 - 14	CH3 356	My God, how wonderful thou art
	Isa.	49: 1 - 4, 15 - 16	CH3 676	Hark, my soul
	Luke	21: 14 - 19		

* * *

New life in Christ	Rom.	6: 4 - 11	SGP 72	Living Lord
	Ephs.	4: 17 - 24	CH3 685	I am trusting thee, Lord Jesus

* * *

Occult, ban on	Isa.	8: 16 - 20	MP 126	Jesus the name high overall
	Is.	47: 8 - 15	CH3 495	O Lord our God arise
	Rev.	22: 12 - 17	CH3 494	Thou whose almighty word

* * *

Peace	Ps.	46	CH3 109	Spirit of God
	Luke	1: 67 - 80	SGP 62	Lead us, O Father

	Rom.	5: 1 - 11	CH3 395	Father of peace
	Ephs.	6: 10 - 18	CH3 322	Thy kingdom come, O God
	Phil.	4: 4 - 9	SGP 76	Make me a channel
	Cols.	3: 12 - 17	MP 538	Peace I give to you

* * *

Prayer	Matt.	6: 5 - 15	CH3 451	Almighty Father
	Luke	11: 1 - 13	SGP 115	What a friend
	Luke	18: 1 - 14	CH3 667	Approach my soul

* * *

Prisoners	Ps.	107: 1 - 3, 10 - 16, 43	CH3 160	Hark the glad sound
	Matt.	25: 31 - 40	SGP 118	Will you come and follow me
	Luke	4: 16 - 21	CH3 413	Jesus shall reign
	Hebs.	13: 1 - 3		

* * *

Reconciliation	Rom.	5: 1 - 11	MP 248	To God be the glory
	Ephs.	2: 11 - 22	SGP 29	For the healing of the nations
			CH3 380	Man of sorrows

* * *

Salvation	Luke	8: 11 - 15	SGP 22	Colours of day
	John	3: 14 - 16	CH3 293	The Saviour died
	Acts	16: 25 - 34	CH3 101	Give praise and thanks
	Rom.	10: 5 - 13	CH3 530	Blest be the everlasting God

* * *

Service	Ex.	3: 1 - 12	CH3 428	Lord of creation
	Isa.	6: 1 - 8	CH3 462	Take my life
	Matt.	20: 25 - 28	CH3 436	O Master, let me walk
	John	13: 12 - 15	SGP 21	Christ's is the world

* * *

| Standards | Ex. | 20 : 1 - 4, 7 - 8, 12 - 17 | CH3 87 | Be thou my vision |
| | Ephs. | 4: 1 - 6 | CH3 434 | O Jesus, I have promised |

* * *

Studying Scripture	Neh.	8: 1 - 3, 5 - 6, 9 - 12	CH3 129	Look upon us, blessed Lord
	Mark	4: 14 - 20	CH3 635	Almighty God
	2 Cor.	4: 1 - 6	MP 316	Break thou the Bread of Life

* * *

| Teaching | Deut. | 11: 1, 18 - 21 | CH3 213 | It fell upon a summer day |
| | Matt. | 18: 1 - 7 | CH3 447 | Lord and Master who has called us |

* * *

| Temptation | Luke | 4: 1 - 13 | CH3 482 | Yield not to temptation |
| | James | 1: 12 - 18 | CH3 211 | Jesus calls us |

* * *

Thanksgiving	1 Chr.	16:	8 - 11	CH3	29	To render thanks
	Ephs.	1:	3 - 8	CH3	366	Sing to the Lord
	Phil.	4:	4 - 7	CH3	368	Now thank we all our God

* * *

| Unity | John | 17: | 1 - 26 | SGP | 13 | Bind us together |
| | | | | CH3 | 424 | Thy hand, O God, has guided |

* * *

Wisdom	Matt.	25:	1 - 13	MP	58	Give me oil
	Luke	2:	41 - 52	CH3	144	God is love
	James	3:	13 - 18	CH3	88	God of grace

WORSHIP
SAMPLER

The worship sampler gives a selection of patterns of worship, with scripture readings, hymns or songs and prayers. They can be used as they stand, or better still, they can be adapted and used as a springboard for your own ideas.

The selection begins with a series of worship patterns. Each one explores a fruit of the spirit as outlined in Galatians 5: 22 – 'But the Spirit produces love, joy, peace, patience, kindness, goodness, faithfulness, humility and self-control'. This series could be followed for a number of meetings, giving a theme to the worship. Other Bible passages which lend themselves to similar use include The Lord's Prayer, The Ten Commandments, Love Is … (1 Corinthians 13) or the Armour of God (Ephesians 6).

Also included is worship for the different seasons of the Guild Year as well as for contemporary issues.

The important thing is to use this selection as a resource and an inspiration, experiment with format and presentations, develop a style which feels comfortable, and enjoy the worship!

The Fruit of the Spirit is ... Love

Introduction

Israel, the Lord who created you says,

> Do not be afraid for I have redeemed you.
> I have called you by your name – you are mine.

> *~ Isaiah 43: 1, 2 (JB) ~*

Hymn: SGP   24   Do not be afraid

Reading: Hosea 11: 1 - 4 (JB)

When Israel was a child I loved him, and I called him out of
  Egypt.
But the more I called to them, the further they went from me;
they have offered sacrifice to the Baals and set their offerings
  smoking before the idols.
I myself taught Ephraim to walk,
I took them in my arms;
yet they have not understood that I was the one looking after
  them.
I led them with reins of kindness, with leading-strings of love.
I was like someone who lifts an infant close against the cheek;
stooping down to him I gave him his food.

Prayer:

God, you are Father and Mother to us all.
And you love us.
Your love is patient and kind,
Your love is not jealous or conceited or proud.
Your love is not ill-mannered or selfish or irritable,
Your love does not keep a record of our wrongs.
Your love is not happy with evil, but is happy with the truth.
Your love never gives up, and the faith, hope and patience of
    your love never end.
Your love was there for us from the beginning, like the love of
    a mother for her child in the womb.
Your love is tender; and nurtures us.
Your love is strong; and dares anything to save us.
Your love is ample; and transforms us into the likeness of Christ.
As a child learns to love from loving parents, help us so to
    learn.
Grant us the grace to grow in this love, revealed to us through
    Jesus Christ.   *Amen.*

Closing Hymn: CH3 115   Come down O Love Divine

... Joy and Peace

Hymns: CH3 92 Lord of all hopefulness, Lord of all joy
                SGP 89 Oh, the love of my Lord
                SGP 76 Make me a channel of your peace

Reading: Galatians 5: 22

Place a free standing cross on your table. Play two minutes of a tape of *joyful* singing followed by two minutes of a tape of the sounds of water. (The Royal National Lifeboat Institution has produced two very good ones). Use a battery as a 'visual aid'. Point out that it has a negative and positive end and both are necessary for it to do its job. Joy is often seen as active, and peace as the opposite. Emphasise that both are needed for our spiritual well-being, if we are to function properly as Christians.

Reading: John 16: 19 - 22

Prayer:

Almighty God, how joyfully we can turn to you – joyful because you have given us hope, a reason for living, peace in our hearts and a risen, living Saviour to follow.

We thank you and pray for those who show your joy in what appears to us to be negative circumstances
 – those who are disabled, mentally or physically
 – those who are poor and deprived
 – those who mourn.

Thank you Lord for your Holy Spirit – the spirit that puts a new song on our lips and new joy in our hearts, and blesses us with the peace that passes all human understanding.   *Amen.*

... Patience and Kindness

Hymn: SGP 111   We are one in the Spirit

Reading 1:   Colossians 1: 10 - 12 (NEB)

We pray that you may bear fruit in active goodness of every kind, and grow in the knowledge of God. May he strengthen you, in his glorious might, with ample power to meet whatever comes with fortitude, patience, and joy; and to give thanks to the Father who has made you fit to share the heritage of God's people in the realm of light.

Reading 2:   2 Samuel 9: 1 - 3, 7 (NEB)

David asked, 'Is any member of Saul's family left, to whom I can show true kindness for Jonathan's sake?' There was a servant of Saul's family named Ziba; and he was summoned to David. The king asked, 'Are you Ziba?', and he answered, 'Your servant, sir'. So the king said, 'Is no member of Saul's family still alive to whom I may show the kindness that God requires?' 'Yes,' said Ziba, 'there is a son of Jonathan still alive; he is a cripple, lame in both feet.'

Prayer:

Gracious, loving God, your patience and kindness are infinite. Christ showed both in the loving way he dealt with those in need; in the way he dealt with the seeming inability of his disciples to understand or believe the evidence of their own eyes. In all their failures and betrayal, he showed patience and kindness.

Let us pause for a moment:

Think about those who make you impatient, those to whom it is difficult to be kind. Think how you show restraint in public, then 'take it out' on those nearest to you who may not understand why. Think of how lack of thought, inconsiderate words and actions may have caused hurt and bitterness.

(*silence*)

Forgive us and help us to show patience and kindness to others for the sake of Jesus. Love is patient, love is kind. Grant us your love in our lives through the power of the Holy Spirit. In Jesus' name.   *Amen.*

Hymn: SGP   71   (verses 1, 3, 5)
              Lord God, your love has called us here

The Grace.

... Goodness

Hymns: SGP 98   Spirit of the living God
                CH3 388   The King of Love my Shepherd is
                CH3 395   Father of Peace, and God of Love

Think of Holman Hunt's picture 'The Light of the World', and imagine that big lamp shining into the innermost parts of your being. Probably, like me, you will be conscious of the dirty bits that you do not want to be exposed, and would wish to hurry up with the cleaning process – or put out the light!

Reading: Ephesians 5: 8 - 14 (NIV)

But you were once darkness but now you are light in the Lord. Live as children of light (for the fruit of the light consists in all goodness, righteousness and truth). Have nothing to do with the fruitless deeds of darkness, but rather expose them. For it is shameful even to mention what the disobedient do in secret. But everything exposed by the light becomes visible. This is why it is said, 'Wake up! O sleeper, rise from the dead, and Christ will shine on you'.

Prayer:

Jesus, Light of the world, help us not to fear your light, but rather to welcome it so that we may quickly clear out even the smallest speck that keeps us from being clean and good.

... Faithfulness

This is part of a letter. Imagine it is to you from an older Christian friend (3 John 2 - 6, NIV):

Dear friend, I pray that you may enjoy good health and that all may go well with you, even as your soul is getting along well. It gave me great joy to have some brothers come and tell about your faithfulness to the truth and how you continue to walk in the truth. I have no greater joy than to hear that my children are walking in the truth.

Dear friend, you are faithful in what you are doing for the brothers, even though they are strangers to you. They have told the church about your love.

When you consider your commitments – as an elder, perhaps, or Sunday School teacher, as a woman in the home or a worker elsewhere – do you think you would deserve a letter like that?

Prayer:

We praise you, Lord, for your love for us, and we praise you for your Spirit within us. Forgive us that we often fail you and live fruitless lives because we don't let him take over.

We thank you for our duties in our homes, churches and neigh-

bourhoods, and ask your Spirit to keep us sensitive to the needs
of others and ready to help with work, deed or company.

In this age of shoddy workmanship and instant results, keep
us faithful and fruitful 'doing all things heartily, as to the Lord',
that we may be your 'good and faithful servants'.

Hymn: CH3 431   Jesus, Master, whose I am.

... Humility
and Self-control

Reading: Mark 9: 33 - 37 (GNB)

They came to Capernaum, and after going indoors Jesus asked his disciples, 'What were you arguing about on the road?'

But they would not answer him, because on the road they had been arguing among themselves about who was the greatest. Jesus sat down, called the twelve disciples and said to them, 'Whoever wants to be first must place himself last of all and be the servant of all'.

Then he took a child and made him stand in front of them. He put his arms round him and said to them, 'Whoever welcomes in my name one of these children, welcomes me and whoever welcomes me, welcomes not only me but also the one who sent me.'

Prayer:

Lord, you've done it again –
...... turned the values of the world upside-down,
...... chosen weakness, in human eyes, as a source of strength,
...... reversed the usual order of things which puts self first,
...... challenged us to forget our self-importance
and follow the way of love
– as you did.

Father, give us grace
...... to speak the truth with childlike simplicity,
...... to understand the truth with childlike directness,
...... to welcome the call to service with childlike eyes
    which see only the need
    without thought of self-righteousness.

Hymn: CH3 76 (verse 1)

> Dear Lord and Father of mankind,
> Forgive our foolish ways;
> Reclothe us in our rightful mind;
> In purer lives thy service find,
> In deeper reverence, praise.

Reading:

'Lord, the anger's there however much I may deny it. I use the Christian cliches, speak of love and service, walking second miles. But still it's there.

'Resentment, irritation, when things don't go my way. The bitter comment, smoke-screened with a smile, disguised as disappointment.

'But underneath I'm seething. Forgiveness stored away in same locked cupboard of my mind. Unopened, and the key misplaced.

'Lord, won't you force the door?

'But even as I ask, I know the answer lies with me. It lies with me to make a move, to recognise just where I'm at and why. And then to work with you towards that partnership of love, not forced but freely given, that casts out fear.'

~ Eddie Askew[9] ~

Prayer:

Lord Jesus Christ,
You have given us the perfect example of self-control.
When the disciples were slow to understand, you were patient.
When the sick crowded round with their incessant demands,
    you gave your healing power freely.
When false accusations were brought against you, you kept
    silence.
When men nailed you to the cross, you forgave them.

Holy Spirit, enter our hearts now
to teach us humility and self-control,
so that anger will be subdued by patience,
irritation will be replaced by generosity,
hurt will give way to that love which endures.

Hymn: CH3 76 (verse 5)

> Drop thy still dews of quietness
> Till all our strivings cease,
> Take from our souls the strain and stress
> And let our ordered lives confess
> The beauty of thy peace.

SAMPLE PATTERNS
... Beginnings

Hymn: CH3 432   May the mind of Christ my Saviour

Readings from: John 1: 1 - 14;
                        Hebrews 13: 1 - 8;
                        Ezekiel   36: 24 - 28

Prayer:

Heavenly Father, for your wonderful work, the Bible, and all the promises it contains, we praise and thank you. We marvel at your great love and mercy. We thank you for all new beginnings, but especially for the beginning of our journey of faith. You know each one of us so well – our shortcomings, doubts and fears – forgive us Lord. Help the seed of faith you have planted to flourish and bear fruit. For those who have not yet begun to understand and trust you, we pray that your light and love will flood their lives.

Lord, fill us with newness of life that we may live our lives constantly praying and rejoicing in you our Saviour, the Alpha and Omega of us all.

Amen.

... Caring

'If our love for Christ were stronger, richer, deeper, we would not calculate so closely how much we can afford to give or do. Love in its supreme moment does not stop at a little. It does not weigh, measure, calculate or restrain, its impulses.'

~ *SPAN*[10] ~

Hymn: SGP 54 Jesus calls us here to meet him

Reading: Matthew 9: 9 - 13 (NEB)

As he passed on from there Jesus saw a man named Matthew at his seat in the custom-house; and he said to him, 'Follow me'. And Matthew rose and followed him. When Jesus was at table in the house, many bad characters – tax-gatherers and others – were seated with him and his disciples. The Pharisees noticed this and said to his disciples, 'Why is it that your master eats with tax-gatherers and sinners?' Jesus heard them and said, 'It is not the healthy that need a doctor, but the sick. Go and learn what that text means, "I require mercy, not sacrifice." I did not come to invite virtuous people, but sinners'.

Prayer:

Loving God, we give you praise and thanks that in the life and deeds of Jesus we see what you are like. We thank you that when he called Matthew, he chose one who in the eyes of religious Jews was an outcast, someone 'Beyond the pale'. Forgive us that even as we claim to love and serve you, we are making judgments based on prejudice and bigotry, lack of knowledge, on colour, class or appearance. Help us to see Christ there, alongside those in our society who are outcasts, people who need our care, our loving concern. Help us to listen so that we hear what is really being said, and not what we've already decided it is. Help us to speak out against injustice and wrong-doing. Caring takes courage, commitment, sacrifice. Strengthen our love so that we do not 'weigh, measure, calculate or restrain its impulse'. In the name of Jesus.

Hymn: SGP   21   Christ's is the world in which we move

Closing Prayer:

Go with us into your world, to see it through your eyes, and to love it as your Spirit enables us.

Amen.

... Celebration

It's great to have something to celebrate: perhaps the opening of a new building, a special anniversary, or even just the start of a new session. And it's good to be able to share our joy in our worship.

Praise: SHF   69   Come on and Celebrate
                 SGP 120   You shall go out with joy
                 CH3   39   Praise to the Lord, the Almighty

Reading: Psalm 150 (GNB)

Praise God in his Temple!
      Praise his strength in heaven!
Praise him for the mighty things he has done.
      Praise his supreme greatness.

Praise him with trumpets.
      Praise him with harps and lyres.
Praise him with drums and dancing.
      Praise him with harps and flutes.
Praise him with cymbals.
      Praise him with loud cymbals
Praise the LORD, all living creatures!

      Praise the LORD!

Prayer: O Lord our God,
Now the times are filled full
Now is the day of wholeness
Now is your place within mankind
Now the time of liberation has arrived
Now is the celebration of the Kingdom.

Amen.

~ Author unknown ~

... Communication

FOR THE CHRISTIAN, COMMUNICATION IS ACTIVE LOVE.

LET US IN SILENCE THINK OF THOSE TO WHOM WE HAVE LISTENED TODAY. WHAT DID WE HEAR?

LET US IN SILENCE THINK OF WHAT WE HAVE HEARD GOD SAY TO US TODAY.

Prayer:

Lord Jesus, you always heard what people were really saying. You heard the pain behind the mask of words. Forgive us that the voice we most like to hear is our own. Help us to develop a listening ear that we may be able to support friends and neighbours in any kind of need. Help us in this to be like Jesus.

WE COMMUNICATE BY TOUCH.

Let us in silence think of those we have touched today. A handshake, a hug, an embrace; or perhaps, in anger, a slap or rebuff.

Prayer:

Lord, your touch was always therapeutic ... it never repelled or hurt. Help us to offer the touch of compassion, the hand of friendship, the hug of encouragement, the embrace of love, so that we affirm one another and share the love of Christ with others.

WE COMMUNICATE BY SPEAKING.

Let us remember in silence what we have said today.
Are there things we wish we had left unsaid?
Are there times we have been silent when we should have spoken?
Are there words of encouragement, support and love to recall?

Prayer:

Lord, we communicate with you in prayer with our words. May they not be meaningless and empty. We want our communication with you to be real. So, Lord, may our words flow from hearts of love and be backed up by action so that we may not only be in touch with you, but communicate your love to others.

WE COMMUNICATE BY GIVING.

The greatest act of communication was on the cross. Jesus gave himself utterly for us so that we might make contact in a real way with God. Let us think in silence of ways in which we can serve others and give ourselves to them.

Prayer:

Lord, we worship you for your total selfless act of love. We can never repay you or thank you adequately. We can only marvel at being the children who receive such boundless love. Fill us with such joyous response that we share this love in serving others that our whole lives may speak of you.

Amen.

Hymns: SGP   2   A new commandment
              SGP 60   Fill us with your love

... Family

Hymns: SGP 13 Bind us together, Lord
               CH3 522 Our Father, by whose name

Readings: Matthew 7: 7 - 13;
            Acts   10: 1 - 8; Psalm 68: 4 - 6

Prayer:

Ever present Father, we come to you as your children, members of your family. We thank you for our Saviour who came as a baby and grew up in a family. Father, we thank you for our homes, for the people who raised us and for the wider family of your church. We praise you for the privilege of becoming your children through faith in Jesus. And so we pray for the children of today who so desperately need to know you and grow in your loving care. Forgive us Lord when we fail to communicate your love for us all.

We ask you to intervene where families are in trouble – where there is no love, comfort and guidance. Keep us mindful of our own blessings and help us to share them in your service. Today we trust you as our heavenly Father and commit ourselves to Jesus as our Saviour and Lord. We pray this in the name of your own dear Son who gave himself willingly so that we might call you Abba, Father. *Amen.*

... Grief/Loss

Introduction

Life begins in loss. In the very act of birth we lose the comfort and security of our mother's womb and are forced out to face a strange and unfamiliar world. The act of birth is inseparable from the pain of letting go. That experience of loss and new birth continues life-long.

When we think of loss we tend to think of the aching grief of losing a loved one in death. But loss, and grief, play a larger part in our lives. We leave people and places and are left by them. We may lose our opportunities, our dreams, our hopes. There are times we may feel we have lost ourselves, our identities, the person we long to be. We may lose our health suddenly, or as we age we may lose our eyesight, our hearing, our mobility – our waistline! We may know the grief of being separated from each other by distance or disagreement.

Whatever our loss, our grief can be great.

Meditative Prayer:
(To be spoken by one, two or four people
and an explanation given that silence will be used).

Voice 1: Living, loving God, our Parent who cares. We bring to you now in the silence, any loss, any grief, large or small, deserved or undeserved, expected or unexpected.

(*pause*)

Voice 2: We have lost those we loved Lord. We are separated and sometimes feel full of anger and confusion yet so alone and empty. The future has changed. No one truly understands. We lift our thoughts and feelings to you.

SILENCE (*at least 10 seconds*)

Voice 3: We lose our health Lord. We feel cheated as body and mind fail us. We face restricted lives, and the shackles of ill-health are irksome and heavy. We lift our thoughts and feelings to you.

SILENCE (*at least 10 seconds*)

Voice 4: We have lost ourselves, the people we long to be. We live lives of lies and have lost our way. We lift our thoughts and feelings to you.

SILENCE (*at least 10 seconds*)

Voice 1: Healing God, take our grief, share our pain, ease its rawness and ache. May the oil of your love and understanding bring balm to our troubled spirits.

Only crushed wheat can be made into bread. Only trampled grapes can be made into wine. May our sometimes crushed and trampled lives be made into something beautiful and worthwhile.

Amen.

Reading:

Whatever we lose or suffer in life let us remember ....

Who shall separate us from the love of Christ? Shall trouble or hardship or persecution or famine or nakedness or danger or sword? .... No, in all these things we are more than conquerors through him who loved us. For I am convinced that neither death, nor life, neither angels nor demons, neither the present nor the future, nor any powers, neither height nor depth, nor anything else in all creation, will be able to separate us from the love of God that is in Christ Jesus our Lord.

~ Romans 8: 35, 37 - 39 (NIV) ~

Comment:

We have the choice. We can remain in our hurt, or with human and divine help we can accept, adapt, change and grow. Even in the most devastating loss we can find the opportunity to create something new, so that the loss need not be futile. As the act of birth is inseparable from the pain of letting go, so in the pain of letting go, we can find new birth.

Hymns: SGP 21 Christ's is the World
             CH3 677 O Love that will not let me go

... The Media

This is based on the Hymn, 'May the mind of Christ my Saviour' (CH3 432). It can be used by two people, one leading prayer, the other reading and all the verses should be sung by everyone.

The Media

TV, radio, newspapers, video, film ... our age is bombarded by the media in all its forms. We are inevitably touched and influenced by it. As Christians we respond by positively affirming the good and beneficial and by discerning and rejecting the bad.

Let us thank God for the freedom and ability to use our minds and apply our understanding to discern the truth in all media presentations.

Read Hebrews 8: 10 (NIV):

> This is the covenant I will make with the house of Israel after that time, declares the Lord. I will put my laws in their minds and write them on their hearts. I will be their God and they will be my people.

Philippians 4: 8, 9 (NIV):

Finally, whatever is true, whatever is noble, whatever is right, whatever is pure, whatever is lovely, whatever is admirable – if anything is excellent or praiseworthy – think about such things.

Sing together verse 1 of 'May the mind of Christ':

May the mind of Christ my Saviour
Live in me from day to day;
By his love and power controlling
all I do or say.

Prayer:

Lord, we praise you that you are holy, pure and righteous. We thank you that by your Holy Spirit you live within us and by your grace will help us to discern good from bad, pure from corrupt, truth from lies. Guard our minds and grant us wisdom for Christ's sake.

Read Psalm 119: 105 (NIV):

'For your word is a lamp to my feet and a light for my path.'

John 8: 31, 32 (NIV):

Jesus said, 'If you hold to my teaching you are really my disciples. Then you will know the truth and the truth will set you free'.

Sing verse 2:

May the word of God dwell richly
In my heart from hour to hour,
So that all may see I triumph
Only through his power.

Prayer:

Father, we thank and praise you for your word given so
that we might hear and believe. We thank you for Christ
your final word sent to bring life and power. May we claim
that power in our daily lives so that we may become salt
and light to those around us and influence our homes and
communities for good.

Read Philippians 4: 4 - 7 (NIV):

Rejoice in the Lord always. I will say it again Rejoice! Let
your gentleness be evident to all. The Lord is near. Do not
be anxious about anything, but in everything, by prayer
and petition, with thanksgiving, present your requests to
God. And the peace of God which transcends all understanding, will guard your hearts and your minds in Christ
Jesus.

Sing verse 3:

May the peace of God my father
Rule my life in everything,
That I may be calm to comfort
Sick and sorrowing.

Prayer:

Lord, when we see TV news bulletins and read in papers of terrible suffering and agony in the world we are over-whelmed. We feel so helpless. Lord, grant us your peace that we may turn our distress into prayer while doing all we can, acknowledging that your Father's care extends to all your children.

Read 1 Corinthians 13: 1 - 3 (NIV):

If I speak in the tongues of men and of angels, but have not love, I am only a resounding gong or a clanging cym-bal. If I have the gift of prophecy and can fathom all mysteries and all knowledge, and if I have a faith that can move mountains, but have not love, I am nothing. If I give all I possess to the poor and surrender my body to the flames, but have not love, I gain nothing.

Sing verse 4:

May the love of Jesus fill me
As the waters fill the sea;
Him exalting, self abasing,
This is victory.

Prayer:

Lord, love is debased in so much of the media. It is fickle, selfish, lustful. Thank you that your love is so different and sets such a high standard and thank you for every pro-gramme and article which highlights this for us. Bless all

Christian broadcasting and writing that your love may reach out to others.

Read Hebrews 12: 1 - 3 (NIV):

Therefore, since we are surrounded by such a great cloud of witnesses, let us throw off everything that hinders and the sin that so easily entangles, and let us run with perseverance the race marked out for us. Let us fix our eyes on Jesus, the author and perfecter of our faith, who for the joy set before him endured the cross, scorning its shame, and sat down at the right hand of the throne of God. Consider him who endured such opposition from sinful men, so that you will not grow weary and lose heart.

Sing verse 5:

May I run the race before me,
Strong and brave to face the foe,
Looking only unto Jesus
As I onward go.

Prayer:

Thank you Lord for being our companion day by day. Thank you for the enrichment that TV, radio and news-papers bring to life. Thank you that you provide in Jesus Christ the most powerful influence in the world. Stir us up to be active participants ... joyfully contributing to life in the power and love of Jesus.

For his glory we ask all these things.   *Amen.*

... Missed Opportunities

Hymns: SGP   48   I need thee every hour
            CH3   69   Come let us to the Lord our God
                  81   My faith looks up to thee

Reader 1:   'Anyone then who knows the good he ought to do
            and doesn't do it, sins.'
                                        ~ *James 4: 17 (NIV)* ~

Reader 2:   So often we feel miserable when we realise too
            late what we ought to have said or done. Perhaps
            we are aware that we have been distinctly unhelp-
            ful or unkind. We know we've let our Lord down
            yet again and we feel useless – failures – every-
            thing negative.

Reader 3:   Remember Peter? He failed his Lord too and wept
            bitterly. Let's read how Jesus dealt with him.

            [*Reading:* John 21: 15 - 17]

Narrator: When they had finished eating, Jesus said to
            Simon Peter ...

Jesus:	Simon, son of John, do you truly love me more than these?
Peter:	Yes, Lord, you know that I love you.
Jesus:	Feed my lambs.
Narrator:	Again Jesus said ...
Jesus:	Simon, son of John, do you truly love me?
Peter:	Yes, Lord, you know that I love you.
Jesus:	Take care of my sheep.
Narrator:	The third time Jesus said to him ...
Jesus:	Simon, son of John, do you love me?
Narrator:	Peter was hurt because Jesus asked the third time, 'Do you love me?'
Peter:	Lord, you know all things: you know that I love you.
Jesus:	Feed my sheep.
Prayer:	Loving heavenly Father, we thank you for your wonderful forgiving love for each one of us. Thank you for giving us the story of Peter's failure and of how Jesus your Son so tenderly restored him to

a position of trust. Father, when we fall and let you down, and feel really sorry about it, draw us back to yourself, so that you can forgive us, and set us on your way again. Thank you for the reassurance of that verse – 1 John 1: 9 – which reminds us that 'if we confess our sins, you are faithful and just and will forgive us our sins'.

... Relationships

Hymn: SGP 115   'What a friend we have in Jesus'
                      (*Tune:* Scarlet Ribbons)

Reading: Matthew 25: 34 - 40

Give everyone a card from a well shuffled pack of Happy Families cards. Then ask them to find the other members of their
family. Point out that this can only be done by relating to and
communicating with one another. You could ask a member of
'Relate' or another caring society to be your guest speaker.

Prayer:

Lord God, we praise and thank you that we are created in your
image and to live together in unity. Forgive us Lord if we have
been responsible for any disharmony, and help us, through your
Spirit, to put matters right. We bring to you all who endure
broken relationships. Thank you for your promise of healing for
the broken-hearted. May we always look to our Lord Jesus
Christ for the way to live with others. Thank you Lord for the
potential we all have to be brothers and sisters in Christ.

... Salt in Society

Hymn: CH3 485   Lord, speak to me

Reading: Mark 9: 50 (GNB)

Salt is good; but if it loses its saltiness, how can you make
it salty again?
Have the salt of friendship among yourselves, and live in
peace with one another.

* * *

'Switch off the television!

There are too many children past crying
          too many parents past caring
          too many governments past sacrificing:
I loathe to see
to be shown undeniably
that my life is merely
          a drop in the ocean.'

Yet
One drop of dye
changes
all of the mixture

One candle's flame
lights
all round this dark room

One pinch of salt
flavours
all of my casserole

Creator God
give us the courage
to change our world's hue;
Let more of your light
spread out from ourselves
giving back to this planet
the flavour of you.

~ Jane Grayshon[11] *~*

Father, forgive us for the times when we feel useless; when we feel tempted to shut out the world and its problems; forgive us for not trying because we feel there is nothing we can do.

Lord, speak to us now –

Lead us, so that we may guide others to you. Strengthen us, so that we may stretch out a loving hand to those in need. Use us as seems best to you, for in your strength all things are possible. This we ask through Jesus Christ our Lord. *Amen.*

Hymn: SGP 76   Make me a channel of your peace
(*said or sung by all*)

... Wisdom

Hymn: SGP   93   Seek ye first

Reading: Proverb 1: 7 *or* 1 Kings 3: 5 - 14

Place an owl figure or picture of an owl where it can be seen by members. Why was an owl the Greek symbol of wisdom? Could it be because it appears to be always listening? We must teach ourselves to listen to God – therein lies wisdom.

Prayer:

Lord, help us to be still and listen to you – give us ears to hear. Solomon valued wisdom above everything in this life. We praise you for the wonder of this world you have given us and our thirst for knowledge. We have so much to learn – we need to be sensitive to others – forgive us our impatience. Can we be the good listeners our friends and neighbours need? Can we bring peace to their souls with the good news of our Saviour? We ask for your Holy Spirit to help us to be wise in the ways of our Lord and to ever look to him for guidance.

Bless those in positions of authority who teach or have to make momentous decisions. We look to you, Lord, the source of all wisdom.

Christmas

Introduction

No Royal Palace for the infant prince born to save the world.

Jesus, born in a cold, draughty stable.

From those humble surroundings sprang a life that was to enrich us beyond measure. Born for us, a child who would became a ruler who would be called 'wonderful Counsellor', 'Prince of Peace', basing all his power on right and justice.

Hymns: JP   93   See him lying in a bed of straw
                                  (Calypso Carol)
                  CH3 179   See! in yonder manger low

Readings: Luke   1: 26 - 38;
                  Isaiah   9: 2; 6 - 7;   Luke 2: 1 - 21

(*Four voices could be used for the readings*)

Prayer:

Father God,
the people who walked in darkness saw a great light.

Today, as we walk in the shadows we ask that you spread the light of Jesus your Son upon us. As we celebrate the birthday of that Son, we pray that we will remain mindful of the reason for his coming.

The Christmas that everyone sees is late night shopping, crowded streets, toys in windows, turkey, plum pudding and parcels under the tree.

Let us remember, as we wonder at the sparkle of tree lights and tinsel, that a little child came into our lives to shed his light upon us, not just at Christmas but until the end of time.

Hymn: CH3 172   O little town of Bethlehem

Closing Prayer:

Deep peace of the running wave to you
Deep peace of the flowing air to you
Deep peace of the quiet earth to you
Deep peace of the shining stars to you
Deep peace of the Son of Peace to you.

~ Gaelic Blessing ~

New Year

'I said to the Man who stood at the gate of the year, "Give me a light that I may tread safely into the unknown". And he replied, "Go out into the Darkness and put your hand into the hand of God. That shall be to you better than light and safer than a known way!" So I went forth and finding the hand of God, trod gladly into the night. And he led me towards the hills and the breaking of day in the lone East.'   ~ *M Louise Haskins*[12] ~

Prayer:

Heavenly Father, we come to you at the start of a new year, knowing what has been, knowing your faithfulness to us, knowing you were there to comfort and guide us when times were difficult, knowing you are a God of love and mercy. We confess we have sinned against you in many ways, but we can make a fresh start, for through the death of Jesus we can be forgiven and put right with you. Your hands were nailed to the cross for us Lord. Now you stretch them out to us. Help us to grasp them daily. Only then can we be unafraid of what the future holds. We pray for those who need you – those who are ill, troubled, depressed or just downright weary. Fill them and us, O Lord, with your Holy Spirit and help us always to remember that our times are in your hands.

Hymns: SGP 69 Look forward in faith
             CH3 424 Thy hand, O God, has guided

Lent

During the period of Lent we prepare to commemorate the death and resurrection of our Lord Jesus Christ. Remembering Christ's struggle – the temptations in the wilderness; the loneliness of Gethsemane – we bring to him our own difficulties and concerns as we seek to be 'fashioned to a truer beauty of his hand'.

Opening Praise:

    SGP 114   Were you there when they crucified my Lord?

Reading: Matthew 4: 1 - 11; Luke 22: 39 - 44

Prayer:

Lord Jesus Christ, present with us now,
For all that you have done for us on the cross
For all that you have promised us
What can we offer in exchange?

Our hands are empty
Our hearts are often rebellious
Our faith is smaller than the mustard seed
But with you is mercy and the power to change us.

Let us bring to God the things and the people who concern us.

[People may contribute as they wish; or the leader may list concerns, allowing time for silent prayer. Each prayer may end either with the spoken response:

Lord in your mercy
HEAR OUR PRAYER

or the sung response: Oh Lord hear my prayer (SGP 85)

After the last prayer, the leader concludes.]

Oh Christ, the Master Carpenter,
who at the last, through wood and nails,
purchased our whole salvation.
Wield well your tools in the workshop of your world,
so that we, who came rough-hewn to your bench,
may here be fashioned to a truer beauty of your hand.
We ask it for your own name's sake.   *Amen.*

~ from *A Wee Worship Book*[13] ~

Annual
General Meeting

Opening Hymn: As this is a time for looking back and planning the way forward, it is appropriate to begin with such hymns as:

     SGP   37   Great is thy faithfulness
     CH3 366   Sing to the Lord a joyful song
     CH3   29   To render thanks unto the Lord

Reading: Colossians   3: 12 - 17
     or Ephesians   4:   1 - 12
     or Romans   12:   4 - 13

Prayer: Dear Father, we came into your presence with grateful and thankful hearts for all your goodness to us. We look back over a busy year in our Guild Branch and thank you for all the happy times we have shared and for all that we have learned of the work of your church.

We ask your blessing on those who are not with us tonight. May they know that we are thinking of them, and that you are near to them.

Accept our thanks for those who have held office throughout the past year, and help each one of us to be ready to serve you in any way we can knowing that you will give us the strength to answer your call.

You have helped us so abundantly Lord. Forgive us that so often we take you for granted and help us to show our thankfulness in the lives we live.

Be with us now as we turn our minds to the business of the meeting, and help us to remember that all we do is for you, our loving heavenly father. *Amen.*

Closing Hymn: SGP   90 One more step along the world I go
                  CH3 462 Take my life, and let it be
                  CH3 428 Lord of Creation, to thee
                              be all praise

Closing Prayer: Father, we commit into your hands the work of this night. Accept our thanks for the sense of your presence and for the joy we have felt. Be with those taking office for the first time. May they prove your faithfulness to them as they seek to serve you. For all who have accepted the responsibility of office, we thank you Lord and ask upon them your blessing. Be with us now as we go our separate ways. Keep us mindful of your loving presence and help us to share with our neighbours the love you have shown to us. In Jesus' name, we ask it. *Amen.*

'Whose I am
and Whom I Serve'

As this is the motto of the Woman's Guild, you may wish to have it displayed in your meeting place.

Hymns: SGP 119   You are worthy
             CH3 445   Make me a captive, Lord
             CH3 412   Will your anchor hold?

Try to imagine yourself involved in the following situation:

Reading: Acts 27: 13 - 26 (NIV)

[Use two voices: Narrator and Paul]

When a gentle south wind began to blow, they thought they had obtained what they wanted; so they weighed anchor and sailed along the shore of Crete. Before very long, a wind of hurricane force, called the 'Northeaster', swept down from the island. The ship was caught by the storm and could not head into the wind; so we gave way to it and were driven along. As we passed to the lee of a small island called Cauda, we were hardly able to make the lifeboat secure. When the men had hoisted it aboard, they passed ropes under the ship itself to hold it together. Fearing that they would run aground on the sand-bars of Syrtis, they lowered the sea anchor and let the ship be driven along. We took such a violent battering from the storm that the next day they began to throw the cargo overboard. On the third day they threw the ship's tackle overboard with their own hands. When neither sun nor stars appeared for many days and the storm continued raging, we finally gave up all hope of being saved.

After the men had gone a long time without food, Paul stood up before them and said, 'Men you should have taken my advice not to sail from Crete; then you would have saved yourselves this damage and loss. But now I urge you to keep up your courage, because not one of you will be lost; only the ship will be destroyed. Last night an angel of the God whose I am and whom I serve stood beside me and said, "Do not be afraid, Paul. You must stand trial before Caesar; and God has graciously given you the lives of all who sail with you". So keep up your courage, men, for I have faith in God that it will happen just as he told me. Nevertheless we must run aground on some island.'

Note how your fear ebbed when Paul took command, proclaiming the reason for his confidence.

Read again verses 23 and 24:

> 'Last night an angel of the God *whose I am and whom I serve* stood beside me and said, "Do not be afraid, Paul".'

Paul believed God and acted on his belief. Note how his fellow travellers reacted to the tone of authority and allowed him to take command. Paul's total commitment to God gave him total confidence in God.

Is our belief in God so strong that we 'serve' him by speaking and acting with confidence in his name? Let us think about our commitment.

Read Romans 12: 1 (NIV):

> Therefore I urge you, brothers, in view of God's mercy, to offer your bodies as living sacrifices, holy and pleasing to God – this is your spiritual act of worship.

When last did you make a sacrifice to God – of time, money, energy, praise or whatever?

(*Pause for a time of silent worship*)

Prayer:

Father God, when we think of your wonderful love for us shown so perfectly in Jesus, surely our response should be like Paul's. Help us Lord to make that decision and give our whole selves over to you, to use as you will. Then we too will have our confidence in the God 'whose we are and whom we serve'.

Epilogue
for World Mission

This could follow an illustrated talk on the work of one of our missionary partners, or a part of the world where the church has a particular concern. The final slide, which should be meaningful, depicting perhaps some needy aspect of the work or a peaceful sunset, should remain on the screen as a focal point; and with the lights still dimmed read a few verses from the Bible, *eg* Ephesians 3: 14 - 21.

Prayer:

God, our Father, you have called us to be intercessors for your work in the world, and you have taught us that prayer is without limits or bounds and is understood by people of every language and creed. We pray for people everywhere, especially for Christians who are, even now, being persecuted for their faith. Give to them, our Father, a sense of your presence with them and grant them courage to withstand the difficulties they may have to endure. We pray for all who have answered your call to be witnesses in countries that are far from home and family. May they experience joy and fulfilment in their work, knowing that they have been obedient to your call and that you are ever present with them to direct and uphold and further your work.

[Insert here two sentences concerning the work and personnel shown on the slides.]

Our Father, as we pray for your people engaged in your work overseas, we ask that we might be ever mindful of the tasks they do in your name. Keep us faithful in our support and in our prayer, so that they and we together may be the means of spreading your love, your joy and your saving grace, through Jesus Christ our Lord.

Amen.

Hymns:	SGP 2	A new commandment
	SGP 29	For the healing of the nations
	SGP 41	Help us accept each other
	CH3 500	Christ for the world we sing!

An Epilogue with a Challenge

The following could be used as a Meditation or a Prayer:

As we think of today's world, we would agree that it is a shrinking world; modern technology in travel and communication makes virtually any part of it accessible within hours of departing, and areas of concern are beamed into our living rooms almost the instant they happen. No longer can we turn our backs on the needs of the world, or 'pass the buck' as being someone else's concern. It is laid on our hearts to be mindful of the plight of others, whether on our own doorstep or on the other side of the world.

A long time ago God confronted Isaiah and said, 'Whom shall I send? And who will go for us?' Jesus said, 'As the Father has sent me, I am sending you'.

Today he says to each one of us, 'Go then to all peoples everywhere' – in person, through prayer, by giving or befriending. He calls you and me to be his messengers – Do we hear? Do we go?

He wants people to go to China, to Africa, to South America, to Scotland, to [*your locality*] and into all the world – Do we hear? Do we go?

God doesn't call us all to be preachers, teachers, pastors or evangelists, but we are all called to be his witnesses. We are called to give evidence of his love and saving grace. We are called to give a reason for our faith. We are Christ's ambassadors and he has given us a task – Do we obey? Do we go?

God says to us today, 'Whom shall I send? And who will go for us?'

Amen.

~ adapted from *Life is for Everyone*[14] ~

Hymns: SGP 21   Christ's is the world in which we move
               CH3 494   Thou whose almighty word
               CH3 485   Lord, speak to me

Closing Prayer:

Let us go out into the world in peace to love and to serve the Lord, and may his blessing go with us and remain with us always.   *Amen.*

THE CENTENARY HYMN

(*Tune:* Regent Square, CH3 354)

(1) Worship we our Lord and Father
      As we gather, as we sing
      Praise him, praise him, now and ever
      Bringing glory to our King
          Worship we our Lord and Father
          Bringing glory to our King.

(2) Fellowship we seek and cherish
      Friend with friend and stranger too
      Sharing troubles, joys and pleasures
      Showing love that comes from you
          Fellowship we seek and cherish
          Showing love that comes from you.

(3) Service to the world we offer
      We would wish to play our part
      But we need your strength to aid us
      Give us caring loving hearts
          Service to the world we offer
          Give us caring, loving hearts.

(4)   Teach us to give you the glory
     When we follow in your way
     Worship, fellowship and service
     Are your gifts from day to day
          Teach us to give you the glory
          For your gifts from day to day.

(5)   We your people praise and thank you
     For the blessings that we have
     Glory, honour, now we give you
     Whose we are and whom we serve
          We your people praise and thank you
          Whose we are and whom we serve.

~ Betty Ewart[15] *~*

REFERENCES

1   *Windows of Prayer* is available from the Church of Scotland Department of National Mission at 121 George Street, Edinburgh EH2 4YN.

2   Geoffrey and Judith Stevenson: *Steps of Faith* (Eastbourne: Kingsway).

3   David Adam: *Edge of Glory: Prayers in the Celtic Tradition* (SPCK/ Triangle, 1985).

4   Julian of Norwich: *Revelations of Divine Love* (editions available from Hodder & Stoughton, Penguin Books and Arthur Clarke Books).

5   St Ignatius Loyola: *Spiritual Exercises* (editions available from Hodder & Stoughton and Arthur Clarke Books).

6   David Adam: *Tides and Seasons* (London: SPCK/Triangle, 1989).

7   Freda Rajotte: 'The Tourist's Prayer' from John Carden (comp): *With all God's People: The New Ecumenical Prayer Cycle* (Geneva: WCC Publications, 1989).

8   Rosaleen Murray (Scottish Catholic International Aid Fund). Quoted on the front cover of June – August 1993 edition of Church of Scotland Department of World Mission's *Prayerline*.

9   Eddie Askew: *Breaking the Rules* (Leprosy Mission International).

10   From SPAN, Australian Presbyterian Women, NSW, Australia.

11   Jane Grayshon: *Faith in Flames* (London: Hodder & Stoughton).

12   M Louise Haskins: *The Desert* (*c.* 1908). Quoted by King George VI in his Christmas broadcast 1939.

13   Wild Goose Worship Group: *A Wee Worship Book* (Iona Community).

14   John C Sharp and John Wilson: *Life is for Everyone* (Edinburgh: Saint Andrew Press, 1988).

15   © Betty Ewart, President (1987), the St Marnock's Branch of the Woman's Guild, Kilmarnock.

RESOURCES

General

Adam, David: *Powerlines: Celtic Prayers about Work* (London: SPCK/ Triangle, 1992).

Adam, David: *Tides and Seasons* (London: SPCK/Triangle, 1989).

Askew, Eddie: *Disguises of Love* (Leprosy Mission International, 1983).

Askew, Eddie: *Silence and a Shouting: Meditations and Prayers* (Leprosy Mission International, 1982).

Cassidy, Sheila: *Good Friday People* (London: Darton, Longman & Todd, 1991).

Christian Aid: *A Generous Land.*

Christian Aid: *Lifelines.*

Church of Scotland Department of National Mission: *Windows of Prayer* (available from 121 George Street, Edinburgh, EH2 4YN).

Foster, Richard: *Celebration of Discipline* (London: Hodder & Stoughton, 1989).

Grayshon, Jane: *Faith in Flames* (London: Hodder & Stoughton, 1990).

Huggett, Joyce: *Listening to God* (London: Hodder & Stoughton, 1986).

Huggett, Joyce: *Open to God* (London: Hodder & Stoughton, 1989).

Huggett, Joyce: *Through the Year: Treasury of 365 Daily Readings and Meditations,* Teresa De Bertodano and Derek Wood (eds), (Guildford: Eagle, 1992).

Hughes, Gerard: *God of Surprises* (Darton, Longman & Todd, 1985).

Julian of Norwich: *Enfolded in Love: Daily Readings,* Robert Llewelyn (ed), (London: Darton, Longman & Todd, 1980).

Mello, Anthony de: *One Minute Wisdom* (USA: Doubleday Image, 1985).

Millar, Dorothy and Peter: *Prayers from a Columban House* (1993).

Morley, Janet (ed): *Bread of Tomorrow: Praying with the World's Poor* (SPCK/Christian Aid, 1992).

Perry, Michael (ed): *Dramatised Bible Readings for Festivals* (London: Marshall Pickering, 1991).

Quoist, Michel: *Pathways of Prayer* (Dublin: Gill & Macmillan, 1990).

Sherrard, Mary (ed): *Women of Faith* (Edinburgh: Saint Andrew Press, 1993).

Snowden, Rita: *A Woman's Book of Prayers* (London: Fount, 1986).

Steven, Campbell R (ed): *An Anthology of Hope* (Jamieson & Munro, 1988).

Stewart, Dorothy (ed): *Women of Prayer* (Oxford: Lion, 1993).

Topping, Frank: *Wings of the Morning* (Cambridge: Lutterworth Press, 1987).

Topping, Frank: *Working at Prayer* (Cambridge: Lutterworth Press, 1981).

Wild Goose Worship Group: *A Wee Worship Book* (Iona Community, 1989).

Woolley, John A: *I am with you.*

Woolley, John A: *Why Suffering?*

Drama

Bell, John and Graham Maule: *Wild Goose Prints* (Iona Community).

Lee, David: *Ex Machina: 25 Original Sketches* (London: Marshall Pickering, 1989).

Burbridge and Watts: *Lightning Sketches.*

Burbridge and Watts: *Potter's Clay Drama* (M Video Services).

Burbridge and Watts: *Red Letter Days* (London: Hodder & Stoughton).

Burbridge and Watts: *Time to Act* (London: Hodder & Stoughton).

Netherbow Arts Centre: *Bethlehem and beyond* (4 plays);

Netherbow Arts Centre: *A Bunch of Five;*

Netherbow Arts Centre: *A DIY Guide to Drama Workshops* (bks 1 and 2);

Netherbow Arts Centre: *Plus Three;*

(all available from 121 George Street, Edinburgh, EH2 4YN).

Reference

Bible Society, The: *GNB Topical Concordance.*
Goodrick and Kohlenberger: *NIV Handy Concordance.*
Nelson's Quick Reference: *Bible People and Places.*
Oxford Bible Reader's: *Dictionary and Concordance.*
Wright, Chris: *User's Guide to the Bible.*

Church Hymnary (third edition) (Oxford University Press).
Junior Praise (London: Marshall Pickering).
Mission Praise (London: Marshall Pickering).
Songs and Hymns of Fellowship (Eastbourne: Kingsway).
Songs of God's People (Oxford University Press).